How to Use

LOTUS NOTES 4.5

How to Use
LOTUS
NOTES 4.5

ERICA KERWIEN

Ziff-Davis Press
An imprint of Macmillan Computer Publishing USA
Emeryville, California

Publisher	Stacy Hiquet
Acquisitions Editor	Lysa Lewallen
Development Editor	Margo R. Hill
Copy Editor	Jim Stanley
Technical Reviewer	Wade Ellery
Production Editor	Barbara Dahl
Cover Design	Megan Gandt
Book Design	Dennis Gallagher/Visual Strategies, San Francisco
Page Layout	Janet Piercy
Indexer	Valerie Robbins

Ziff-Davis Press, ZD Press, the Ziff-Davis Press logo are trademarks or registered trademarks of, and are licensed to Macmillan Computer Publishing USA by Ziff-Davis Publishing Company, New York, New York.

Ziff-Davis Press imprint books are produced on a Macintosh computer system with the following applications: FrameMaker®, Microsoft® Word, QuarkXPress®, Adobe Illustrator®, Adobe Photoshop®, Adobe Streamline™, MacLink®Plus, Aldus® FreeHand™, Collage Plus™.

Ziff-Davis Press, an imprint of
Macmillan Computer Publishing USA
5903 Christie Avenue
Emeryville, CA 94608

ISBN 1-56276-513-2

Manufactured in the United States of America
10 9 8 7 6 5 4 3 2 1

TABLE OF CONTENTS

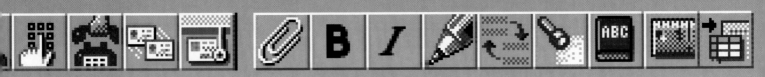

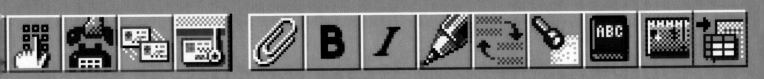

INTRODUCTION

 This book is for computer users who are new to Notes. Notes is unlike most other applications in that it allows you to optimize your communication and collaboration with other computer users. Notes is best described as a workgroup computing environment that helps people to work together regardless of the operating system being used, the organization one belongs to, the location of a user, or their time zone. Notes allows Windows, Macintosh, UNIX, and OS/2 users to share information using the same Notes features, including mail and shared Notes databases. Notes is a client/server application, so to share information with other Notes users in Notes databases and via mail, one or more Notes servers must be accessible on a network. The design and maintenance of Notes servers is left to Notes administrators.

To get the most from Notes, you need a way to connect to a Notes network (a network with one or more Notes servers on it), either through a connection to a Local Area Network within an organization or by being able to dial into a Notes network with a modem. A Notes server (also called Domino) is different from a file server in that it allows an organization to share and replicate data, as well as access the Internet and the World Wide Web. It is up to the organization you belong to, and its Notes administrators and Notes application designers, to take full advantage of the myriad features Notes has to offer; however, all users can use Notes mail, access the Internet, and set up Notes databases to store and track information. This book will show you how to do all this and more.

Each page of each chapter in this book is layed out so that you can learn a concept by following numbered steps in a logical order. The steps are accompanied by graphics to help you visually follow the procedure to accomplish a task, whether the task is to set up Notes, send mail, or edit text.

The tips on each subject add value to the task you are learning. The tips are a combination of advanced information, things to watch out for, side notes on procedures, and tidbits of information that are not directly discussed while following the step-by-step instructions on the page.

There are also three TryIt! sections in this book, strategically located to test skills you have learned in previous chapters, as well as give you ideas on using Notes features, and lead you to take advantage of the features covered in previous chapters. The TryIt! sections, like the chapters, become progressively more challenging to move you forward in your quest to learn how to use Notes.

Notes is a rich user environment that can change the way you work on your own and with your peers. Part of the wonder of Notes is the flexibility and accessibility you have to people and information. You can take advantage of all or part of what Notes has to offer, and you can dive into using it immediately. So don't hold back because it seems like a tremendous application to learn. Set up Notes, learn as you go, and follow the steps! And have fun!

CHAPTER 1

Setting Up Notes

Lotus Notes can be installed on a workstation running Windows, Macintosh, UNIX, or OS/2 operating systems. There is a separate install program for each of these operating systems, so follow the instructions for the operating system you choose.

Once you have installed Notes on your workstation, you can start Notes and step through the setup procedure. Whether you are launching Notes from a PC or a Macintosh computer, the first time you start Notes you will follow a setup procedure to choose what type of Notes server connection you plan on using.

In this chapter you will learn how to set up Notes based on how you plan to connect to a Notes server. There are four possible Notes server connection setups:

▸ You can use Notes while connected to a network (for example, connected to a local area network in your office).
▸ You can use Notes with a modem while you are away from a network (mobile use).
▸ You can use Notes for both network and mobile use.
▸ You can use Notes without being connected to a Notes server.

Once you have completed the Notes setup, you are ready to begin using Notes. In the next chapter you will learn how to customize your Notes settings for startup, basic, mail, and other specific settings.

How to Set Up Notes for Network Use

You set up Notes for network use when your connection to a Notes server is exclusively through a local area network. A common way to use this setup is when a desktop PC is accessing a Notes server from an office with a permanent network connection.

In order to complete this installation, your Notes administrator will either give you a Notes user ID file on a disk, or will make your user ID file available in the Notes Public Name and Address Book. In addition, you will need to know the name of your home server, network type, and your user ID password (if your user ID has been password-protected). If you are unclear about any of these three things, speak to your Notes administrator before continuing with the setup. Otherwise, forge ahead!

TIP SHEET

▶ **Most organizations use hierarchical naming, which means your name will include one or more branches in addition to your name. For example, your full hierarchical name may be "Janet Smith/Sales/Imperial," not just Janet Smith. It is necessary to enter the full hierarchical name during setup. Make sure you enter forward slashes "/" and not back slashes "\."**

▶ **Your location document in your Personal Name and Address Book contains all the information gathered for your connection. To change any of this information, open your Personal Name and Address Book (it will have your name in front of it indicating that it is your Name and Address Book) in the Location view.**

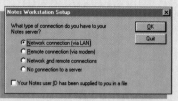

▶ **1** This is the screen you see when you start Notes for the first time. Select the first bullet option, Network Connection (via LAN). Also select the checkbox Your Notes User ID Has Been Supplied To You In A File if you are using a user ID file. Select OK to go on to the next step.

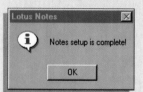

7 The Notes workstation setup is complete! Select OK to begin using Notes.

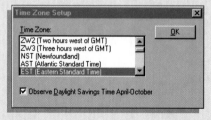

6 Select your time zone in the dialog box.

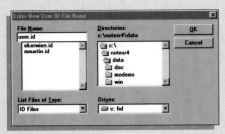

2 When you have your user ID in a file, this dialog box appears asking you to identify your user ID file. Navigate through the drives to find the location of your ID file, whether it is on a floppy disk, your hard drive, or a network drive. Notes will ask you if you want to copy your ID file to your data directory. Select Yes and go to the next step. If you do not have your ID file, skip this dialog box and go on to step 4.

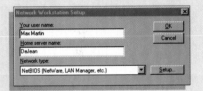

3 Enter the password assigned to your user ID (if one was assigned). You can change the password of your user ID once Notes setup is complete. It is a good idea to password-protect your user ID if you will be the only person using your workstation. Select OK to go to the next step.

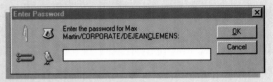

4 Now enter your user name (if it is not automatically filled in) and enter your home server name. Your home server is the Notes server where your mail file is stored. Select the network type if it is a type other than the one listed by default (either TCP/IP or AppleTalk when you are using a Macintosh). Select OK to go to the next step.

5 Notes will now create your Personal Name and Address Book in your Notes data directory (or data folder on the Macintosh), add the Public Name and Address Book and your mail database to your workspace, and enable a location document for your network connection (in your Personal Name and Address Book).

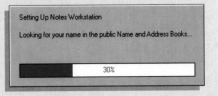

How to Set Up Notes for Mobile Use

You can set up Notes for mobile use when your connection to a Notes server is exclusively through a modem and a dial-up line. A common way to use this setup is while you are traveling with a laptop PC and you want to access a Notes server by dialing into the server over a telephone line.

In order to complete this installation, your Notes administrator will either give you a Notes user ID file on a disk, or will make your user ID file available in the Notes Public Name and Address Book. In addition, you will need to know the name of your home server, your Notes server's phone number, your modem type, any optional phone dialing prefix, and your user ID password (if it has been password-protected). If you are unclear about any of this required information, speak to your Notes administrator before continuing with the setup. Otherwise, onward to setup!

TIP SHEET

▸ **Make sure you have a modem attached to your computer and a modem port enabled before you set up Notes for mobile use. By default, Notes selects the COM1 port as your modem port under Windows and OS/2, the Serial1 port under UNIX, and the Modem port under the Macintosh.**

▸ **You can change the configuration of your modem port after setup by choosing File, Tools, User Preferences, selecting the Ports icon, selecting the Modem port (usually COM1) and then selecting the COM1 Options button.**

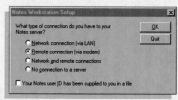

▶ **1** This is the first screen you see when you start Notes for the first time. Select the second bullet option, Remote Connection (via Modem). Also select the checkbox Your Notes User ID Has Been Supplied To You In A File if you are using a user ID file. Select OK to go on to the next step.

8 The Notes workstation setup is complete! Select OK to begin using Notes.

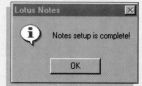

7 Select your time zone in the dialog box.

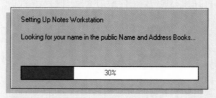

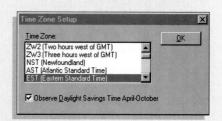

6 Notes will now dial the Notes server and create your Personal Name and Address Book in your Notes data directory (or data folder on the Macintosh), add the Public Name and Address Book and your mail database to your workspace (if you are using Notes mail), create an "Outgoing Mail on Local" database (an outgoing mail box), and enable a location document for your remote connection (in your Personal Name and Address Book).

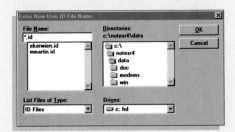

2 When you have your user ID in a file, this dialog box appears asking you to identify your user ID file. Navigate through the drives to find the location of your ID file, whether it is on a floppy disk, your hard drive, or a network drive. Notes will ask you if you want to copy your ID file to your data directory. Select Yes and go to the next step. If you do not have your ID file, skip this dialog box and go on to step 4.

3 Enter the password assigned to your user ID (if one was assigned). You can change the password of your user ID once Notes setup is complete. It is a good idea to password-protect your user ID if you will be the only person using your workstation. Select OK to go to the next step.

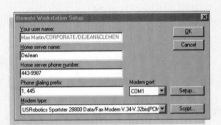

4 Now enter your user name (if it is not automatically filled in) and enter your home server name. Your home server is the Notes server where your mail file is stored. Select a modem type (the brand name and model of your modem) and a modem port. If the name of your modem does not appear on the list, select "Auto Configure (for unlisted modems, only)" from the bottom of the list. Select the Setup button if you would like to change the default settings for the modem port. Otherwise, select OK and go to step 6.

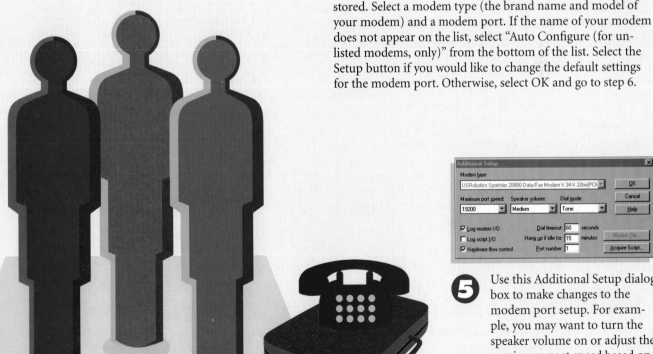

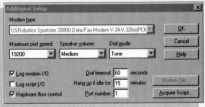

5 Use this Additional Setup dialog box to make changes to the modem port setup. For example, you may want to turn the speaker volume on or adjust the maximum port speed based on the speed of the modem. When you are done, select OK and go to the next step.

How to Set Up Notes for Network and Mobile Use

You can set up Notes for both network and mobile use when you will be using Notes while connected to a local area network as well as through a modem and a dial-up line. A common way to use this setup is when you are in an office part of the time, and travel with a laptop PC the remainder of the time and need to access a Notes server remotely by dialing into the server over a telephone line.

In order to complete this installation, your Notes administrator will either give you a Notes user ID file on a disk, or will make your user ID file available in the Notes Public Name and Address Book. In addition, you will need to know the name of your home server, your Notes server's phone number, your modem type, any optional phone dialing prefix, your network type, and your user ID password (if it has been password-protected). If you are unclear about any of this required information, speak to your Notes administrator before continuing with the setup. Otherwise, onward to complete your setup!

TIP SHEET

▶ If you use TCP/IP as your network type, Notes will ask you for your home server name when the port is first enabled. Your Notes administrator can give you the name to enter so Notes can find your home server. If your network is not using a Domain Name Server you will need to enter the Notes server name and the server's IP address in the host file on your workstation.

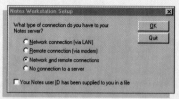

▶ **1** This is the first screen you see when you start Notes for the first time. Select the third bullet option, Network And Remote Connections. Also select the checkbox Your Notes User ID Has Been Supplied To You In A File if you are using a user ID file. Select OK to go on to the next step.

8 The Notes workstation setup is complete! Select OK to begin using Notes.

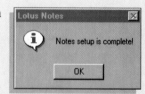

7 Select your time zone in the dialog box.

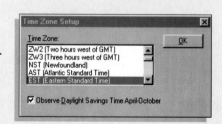

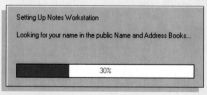

6 Notes will now create your Personal Name and Address Book in your Notes data directory (or data folder on the Macintosh), add the Public Name and Address Book and your mail database to your workspace (if you are using Notes mail), create an "Outgoing Mail on Local" database (an outgoing mail box), and enable a location document for your network and remote connection (in your Personal Name and Address Book).

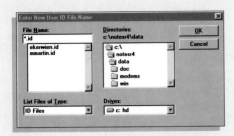

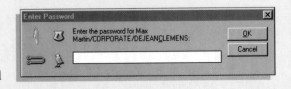

③ Enter the password assigned to your user ID (if one was assigned). You can change the password of your user ID once Notes setup is complete. It is a good idea to password-protect your user ID if you will be the only person using your workstation. Select OK to go to the next step.

② When you have your user ID in a file, this dialog box appears asking you to identify your user ID file. Navigate through the drives to find the location of your ID file, whether it is on a floppy disk, your hard drive, or a network drive. Notes will ask you if you want to copy your ID file to your data directory. Select Yes and go to the next step. If you do not have your ID file, skip this dialog box and go on to step 4.

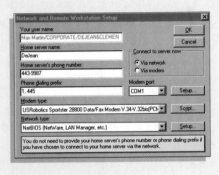

④ Under the Connect To Server Now option at the top right of the dialog box, select either option to connect to a Notes server by network or modem to complete the setup. Now enter your user name (if it is not automatically filled in) and enter your home server name if you will be using Notes mail. Your home server is the Notes server where your mail file is stored. Select a modem type (the brand name and model of your modem) and a modem port. If the name of your modem does not appear on the list, select "Auto Configure (for unlisted modems, only)" from the bottom of the list. Select the Setup button if you would like to change the default settings for the modem port (see step 5). Select the network type if it is a type other than the one listed by default (either TCP/IP or AppleTalk when you are using a Macintosh). Otherwise, select OK and go to step 6.

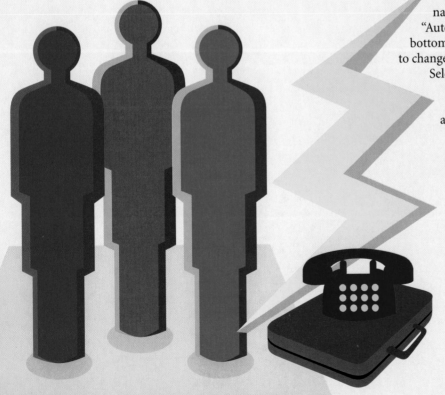

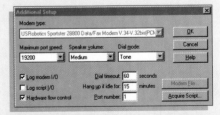

⑤ Use this Additional Setup dialog box to make changes to the modem port setup. For example, you may want to turn on the speaker volume or adjust the maximum port speed based on the speed of the modem. When you are done, select OK and go to the next step.

How to Set Up Notes without a Connection to a Notes Server

You can set up Notes without a connection to a Notes server when the workstation will not have either a network or a modem connection. A common way to use this setup is when you are using a desktop PC or laptop as a stand-alone workstation, or you are temporarily without a network or modem (dial-up) connection and need to complete the setup routine. You can also use this connection type to remotely (dial-up) access a passthru Notes server. This allows you to set up Notes, and then you can manually create connection document(s) to allow you to dial the passthru server, and thereby access other Notes servers. For more on passthru servers, see Chapter 13.

In order to complete this installation, your Notes administrator must give you a Notes user ID file on a disk. This is the simplest of all the Notes setups to complete; however, if you have any problems with this setup contact your Notes administrator.

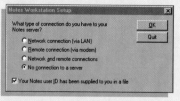

▶ **1** This is the first screen you see when you start Notes for the first time. Select the last bullet option, No Connection To A Server. Also select the checkbox Your Notes User ID Has Been Supplied To You In A File if you are using a user ID file. Select OK to go on to the next step.

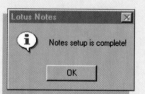

6 The Notes workstation setup is complete! Select OK to begin using Notes.

TIP SHEET

▶ **You can backtrack through setup at almost any point by clicking on the Cancel button in the current dialog box.**

▶ **To exit Notes, choose File, Exit Notes (File, Quit on the Macintosh) or press Alt+F4.**

▶ **To interrupt or stop Notes while it is processing information, press Ctrl+Break (or Command+period on the Macintosh).**

2 When you have your user ID in a file, this dialog box appears asking you to identify your user ID file. Navigate through the drives to find the location of your ID file, whether it is on a floppy disk, your hard drive, or a network drive. Notes will ask you if you want to copy your ID file to your data directory. Select Yes and go to the next step. If you do not have your ID file, skip this dialog box and go on to step 4.

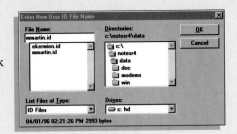

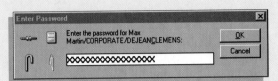

3 Enter the password assigned to your user ID (if one was assigned). You can change the password of your user ID once Notes setup is complete. It is a good idea to password-protect your user ID if you will be the only person using your workstation. Select OK to go to the next step.

4 Now enter your user name if it is not automatically filled in. Select OK and Notes will create your Personal Name and Address Book in your Notes data directory.

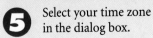

5 Select your time zone in the dialog box.

CHAPTER 2

Customizing Your Settings

 In this chapter you will learn how to adjust a series of settings to optimize your everyday use of Notes. You change Note's settings in the User Preferences dialog box, which is opened by choosing File, Tools, User Preferences. All the settings are saved in a file called NOTES.INI (Notes Preferences file on the Macintosh), which is found in the Windows directory.

There are four categories of settings to select from: Basics, International, Mail, and Ports. Within each of these categories are settings for specific functions, such as what day you want the week to start on, when to lock your ID, which mail program you are using (you can use Notes mail, cc:Mail, another compatible mail program, or no mail), and increasing the volume on your modem port when dialing a Notes server.

Customizing your Notes environment will help you work more efficiently, so take some time to understand how these settings help you do your work. When you are done fine-tuning your Notes settings, the next chapter will teach you how to use the Notes workspace.

How to Choose Startup Settings

Some of the settings in Notes take effect when Notes is first opened, and some of these startup settings (or preferences) trigger some actions when Notes first opens. Others are in effect the entire time Notes is open for that session.

When you change one or more of the startup settings, you will have to exit and then restart Notes to see the settings changes take effect.

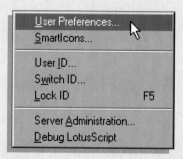

▶ **❶** Choose File, Tools, User Preferences to open the User Preferences dialog box. The first pane, Basic Settings, displays the startup settings.

Wdrop cap on topic spread

❻ If you select the Startup Database button, the Startup Database dialog box appears. Select a database you want Notes to open when you first start Notes. This is useful when you consistently open the same database each time you start Notes, such as your mail database.

TIP SHEET

▶ **The Prompt for Location option is useful when you have more than one location document. Location documents are in your Personal Name and Address Book and allow you to specify whether you are dialing into a Notes server, or accessing a server over a network. Your location setup can be edited either by opening your Personal Name and Address Book to the Location documents, or by selecting a location from the second pop-up menu (from the right) on the Notes status bar (the bottom bar on your Notes screen). For more details on your location information, see Chapter 13, "Using Mobile Notes."**

▶ **When you select the Enable Local Background Indexing option, Notes will also automatically update the full text index of the database after a database replication has occurred. This is useful because otherwise, after replication between databases, data has changed and it would take time to update the indexes before you were able to view the replication changes.**

☐ Scan for unread

2 If you select this option, when Notes starts it will find unread documents in the databases you select to scan. To select databases to scan, close all open databases and deselect all databases on the Notes workspace. Now the Notes workspace is the active window. Choose Edit, Unread Marks, Scan Unread, and select the Choose Preferred button to show a list of the databases on your workspace to select from.

☐ Prompt for location

3 If you select this option, each time Notes starts it will ask you your current location (such as office or remote location). This option is useful when you have two or more locations.

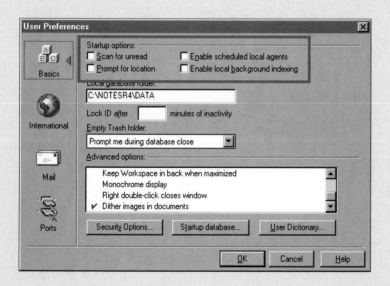

☐ Enable scheduled local agents

4 If you select this option, Notes will run your scheduled agents when you first start Notes. *Scheduled agents* are automated tasks that have been scheduled to run at periodic intervals, such as archiving mail, sending mail, and placing specific documents in a folder.

☐ Enable local background indexing

5 If you select this option, you will be able to create full-text indexes in the background so that you can continue working in Notes while a database's full-text index is being created. This is useful because some indexes take a substantial amount of time to create. The amount of time depends on how much data Notes must index, but on average it can take several minutes.

How to Choose Basic Settings

The basic settings covered here are those settings—apart from the startup and the advanced settings—that appear in the Basic panel of the User Preferences dialog box. The previous topic covered the startup settings, and the next topic covers the advanced settings.

These settings can be changed at any time to reflect how you are currently using a particular feature. The settings here affect how you view and store databases on your local hard drive, how you lock your user ID, how to empty your mail's trash folder, and how you customize your user dictionary.

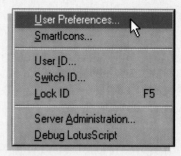

▶ **❶** Choose File, Tools, User Preferences to open the User Preferences dialog box. The first panel of settings, Basic settings, displays the basic settings covered on this page.

W drop cap on topic spread

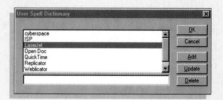

❺ Select the User Dictionary button to view the User Spell Dictionary dialog box. Use this option to add, update, and delete words in your Notes user dictionary. To add a word, type it in the text box at the bottom of the dialog box and then select the Add button. To delete a word, select it from the list and the select the Delete button. To update the spelling of a word, select the word from the list, type in the update in the text box, and select the Update button.

TIP SHEET

▶ **Your NOTES.INI file (or Notes Preferences file on the Macintosh) holds the preferences you set in the User Preferences dialog box. The NOTES.INI file is found in the Windows directory in Windows 3.1 or Windows 95. The Notes Preferences file is found in the Preferences folder in the System folder on the Macintosh.**

▶ **In order for the Lock ID After feature to work, you must password-protect your Notes user ID. Also make sure you remember your ID password before you activate this feature. For more details on securing your Notes desktop, see Chapter 18, "Securing Your Notes Desktop."**

▶ **The user dictionary is a file called USER.DIC, found in your Notes data directory (or Data folder on the Macintosh). The USER.DIC file is not created until the first time you modify the user dictionary in the User Preferences dialog box.**

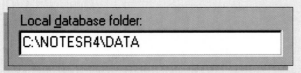

2 This option indicates where your Notes data directory is located. The Notes data directory (or Data folder on the Macintosh) contains your Notes local databases (such as replica databases, your local mail replica, and your Personal Name and Address Book), your DESKTOP.DSK file, and your NOTES.INI file if you are using OS/2 or UNIX operating systems. To change the location of the data directory, either enter a new path in the text box below the Local Database Folder option, or on a Macintosh, select the Browse button to select a Notes data folder. Notes looks for these files, as well as replicating databases, in the designated data directory. In most cases, this data directory path should not be changed.

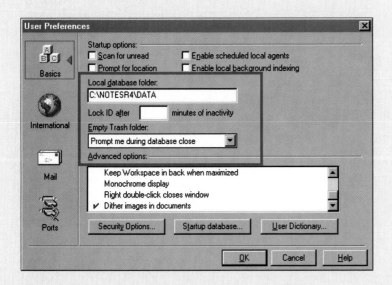

3 Select this option to lock your Notes ID automatically. When Notes has not been used for a specified amount of time, Notes will log you off of any Notes servers you are connected to and ask you for your password in order to access Notes again. This prevents another user from accessing Notes servers with your open Notes client while you are not at your workstation. Enter the number of minutes of inactivity after which Notes will lock your ID.

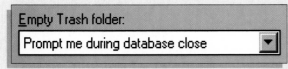

4 Use this option to indicate when and how you want Notes to empty the trash folder in your mail database. The trash folder contains mail you have marked to be deleted from your mail database. There are three options: Prompt Me During Database Close will ask you if you want to delete the mail in the trash folder each time you close your mail database; Always During Database Close will automatically delete the mail in the trash folder each time you close your mail database; Manually will not delete mail from your trash folder—you must do it yourself by choosing Actions, Empty Trash, while in your mail database.

How to Choose Advanced Settings

The Basic panel of the User Preferences dialog box contains a list of advanced settings you should review. Several of the settings apply to how Notes displays the workspace, data, and Internet/Web functionality within Notes databases and documents.

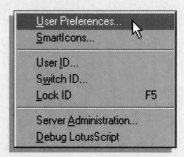

▶ ❶ Choose File, Tools, User Preferences to open the User Preferences dialog box. The first panel of settings, Basic settings, displays the advanced settings in a scroll box in the middle of the dialog box. A checkmark to the left of the advanced option indicates the option is on. To see some of the advanced feature options in this scroll box, you may need to scroll up or down using the vertical scroll bar on the right.

 If you use Windows, OS/2, or UNIX, you have the option of double-clicking the right mouse button to close the active Notes window by selecting Right Double-Click Closes Window. Alternatively, without selecting this option, the right mouse button displays a menu of options relevant to the active window. On the Macintosh, pressing the Option button and clicking the mouse button displays this menu.

TIP SHEET

▶ **Other advanced settings are discussed in later chapters. Workspace settings, in particular, are covered in the Chapter 3.**

When you select the Mark Documents Read When Opened In Preview Pane option, documents you have read in the preview pane of a database are marked read. A document is indicated as read when it no longer has an asterisk next to it (in the left column of the view pane).

❸ When you select the Make Internet URLs (http://...) Into Hotspots option, Notes changes URLs (uniform resource locators, better known as World Wide Web page addresses) into Notes hotspots. This allows you to click on the hotspot to launch the Web page in your Notes Personal or Server Web Navigator. For more about the Web Navigator, see Chapter 19, "Browsing the World Wide Web with Notes."

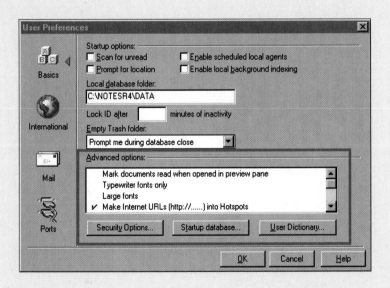

❹ Scroll to find the Don't Show Stored Form Warning option; when you select this option, Notes will not warn you when it opens a document that contains a stored form. Storing a form with a document allows documents to display correctly even if the form for a document is not present in a database.

❺ Scroll to find the Dither Images In Documents option; when you select this option, the display of images that are using 256 colors improves as Notes dithers the image. This process takes more time to display the image and only works with workstations that support 256-color monitors.

❻ You can modify the way Notes displays text in documents using either the Typewriter Fonts Only option, or the Large Fonts option. The Typewriter Fonts Only option displays monospaced text, which is useful when checking tab alignment and columns in documents. The Large Fonts option displays text slightly larger and darker than conventional fonts, and is useful when the default fonts are too small for your monitor.

How to Choose International Settings

The International panel in the User Preferences is where you can specify settings for how Notes sorts characters, units of measurement, character translation, and the language to use to spell-check documents.

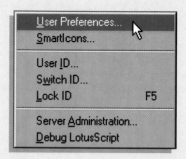

► **1** Choose File, Tools, User Preferences to open the User Preferences dialog box. Select the second panel of settings, International.

► **The American English dictionary file name is LOTUSEN1.DIC. All the language dictionary files have the .DIC file extension and are stored in the Notes program directory. The user dictionary, with the file name USER.DIC, is located in the Notes data directory (or Data folder on the Macintosh).**

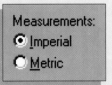

2 This set of options allows you to specify how Notes sorts characters in documents and views. For example, Notes sorts numbers and accented characters first and then letters (alphabetically). Alternatively, you can change the way characters are sorted. Scandinavian Collation sorts some accented characters last. Numbers Last Collation sorts numbers after letters. French Casing removes accent marks from most letters when they are changed from lowercase to uppercase. Note that to sort the documents with the new setting, you must restart Notes and press Shift+F9 to refresh (and thereby re-sort) a view.

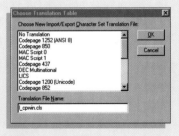

3 Here you can change the unit of measurement currently being used. Although Notes uses inches by default, if you prefer to measure in centimeters you can change this setting. (Imperial uses inches, and Metric uses centimeters.)

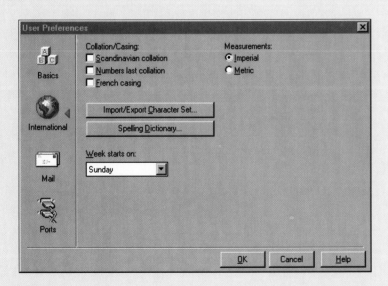

4 Select the Import/Export Character Set button to choose a character translation file to use for importing and exporting data into and out of Notes documents and views. You select a character translation file for Notes to use when you import or export data that contains special characters. (For example, when you use international currency symbols in a file, or use a Macintosh-formatted file with characters unique to the Macintosh character set.)

5 Select the Spelling Dictionary button to open the Choose Dictionary dialog box. Choose a dictionary from the installed Notes dictionaries that suits your language. The default dictionary is the American English dictionary.

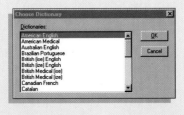

How to Choose Mail Settings

The Mail panel in the User Preferences dialog box is where you can specify mail settings. You can select an alternative mail system or mail file, save sent mail, set your Personal Name and Address Book(s), set a mail notification, electronically sign mail, encrypt mail you send, and encrypt mail you save.

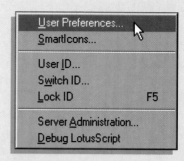

▶ ❶ Choose File, Tools, User Preferences to open the User Preferences dialog box. Select the third panel of settings, Mail.

❽ Select the Encrypt Saved Mail option when you want to encrypt messages (and drafts of messages) that you save while sending your mail.

❼ Select the Encrypt Sent Mail option when you want to encrypt all mail messages you send.

❻ Select the Sign Sent Mail option to electronically sign all mail messages you send. This signature lets recipients know that you created the message.

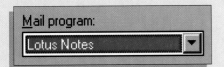

2 You can use Notes mail (or not—in which case None is then selected), or if you are running Windows you can select from cc:Mail or another compatible (VIM) mail program. If you are not sure which mail program you are using, speak to your Notes administrator. To select another mail program, hold down the down arrow button and then select a mail option from the menu options.

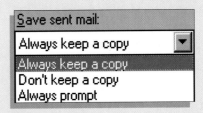

3 Select the pop-up menu for the Save Sent Mail option. You have three choices: Always Keep A Copy (of sent mail), Don't Keep A Copy (of sent mail), or Always Prompt. When Always Prompt is selected, Notes will always ask (prompt) you if you want to save a copy of the mail you are sending.

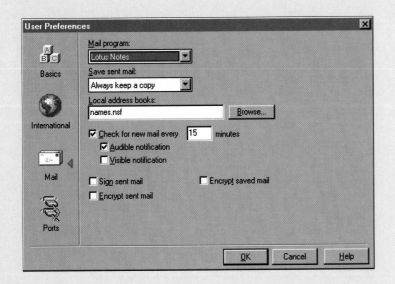

4 This text box is where you enter the file name of your Personal Name and Address Book (the default file name is NAMES.NSF). Notes uses this address book to look up the electronic addresses of people and group names when you are addressing mail. To switch to another address book or add an address book, you can manually type in the file name of the address book in the text box, or use the Browse button to find the address book file and automatically add it to the text box.

5 To indicate that you wish to be updated on incoming mail, select this option and specify the time interval to check for new mail. In addition, you can choose to have an audible notification which sounds like a chime, or visible notification, which displays a dialog box telling you have new mail while Notes is open.

How to Set Up Communication Ports

The last panel in the User Preferences dialog box is the Ports panel. This collection of settings allows you to set up and change the settings for communication ports when connecting with one or more Notes servers, for both network and modem type connections.

In most cases, you will not need to adjust or set up ports because they are configured for you the first time you go through Notes setup. However, in some cases you will want to adjust the settings for a port. For example, you may want to adjust the speed of a modem port.

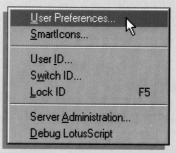

1 Choose File, Tools, User Preferences to open the User Preferences dialog box. Select the fourth panel of settings, Ports.

TIP SHEET

▶ **The order of the ports in the list of communication ports is important when you are using a network connection and have more than one port enabled. Notes will try to establish a connection with a Notes server using the ports in the order they appear in the list; however, enabled ports that are not in use in the current location will not be tried. To see which ports you have enabled for the location, open your current location record either by selecting Edit Current from the status bar menu at the bottom of the Notes desktop, or open the location record in your Personal Name and Address Book.**

▶ **The ports displayed in the list of Communication Ports depends on the operating system you are using. Notes displays some or all of these network ports: LAN0, SPX, VINES, TCP, MacTCP, and AppleTalk. Notes displays one type of the following types of modem ports: COM1 through COM5, or Serial1 through Serial5 (UNIX), or Modem (Macintosh).**

11 Select a port and the Encrypt Network Data option to force Notes to encrypt data sent through a selected port. Enabling this feature slows up the transmission rate slightly.

10 You can enable or disable a port by selecting or deselecting the Port Enabled option.

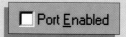

9 To select or deselect additional options on a particular port, select the port and then select the port's Options button.

2 To view settings for a specific port, highlight the port in the list of ports.

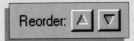

3 Notes uses the ports for a network connection in the order they are listed in this dialog box, but you can reorder the ports so that the port you use the most is listed first. This way Notes will try to connect to a server using the first port, and then try the next port if the first port does not establish a connection.

4 You can add a port by choosing the New button to open the New Port dialog box. Enter the name of the new port, select a driver for the port, and select the locations to use the port. The locations listed are those you currently have created.

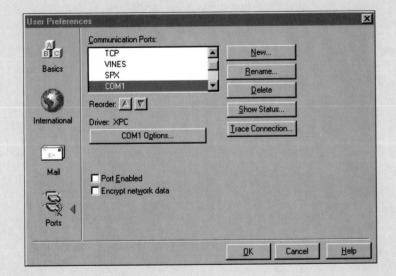

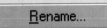

5 To rename a port, select the port to rename from the list of ports, and select the Rename button. In the Rename Port dialog box, enter the new name and select the OK button.

Delete

6 To delete a port, select the port from the list of ports and then select the Delete button. You will not be warned before you delete the port, so be sure you want to take this action!

Show Status...

7 To get information on the current network activity (or remote connection in the case of a modem port) of a port, select the port and then select the Show Status button.

Trace Connection...

8 You can trace the path Notes takes to connect to a server on a network by selecting the Trace Connection button. This is useful when you are troubleshooting problems with a connection to a Notes server.

CHAPTER 3

The Notes Workspace

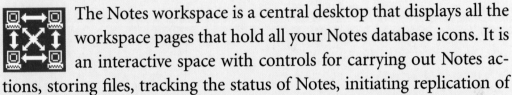 The Notes workspace is a central desktop that displays all the workspace pages that hold all your Notes database icons. It is an interactive space with controls for carrying out Notes actions, storing files, tracking the status of Notes, initiating replication of databases, and keeping your Notes data organized and easily accessible.

This chapter shows you how to customize your workspace to best suit your work and organizational habits. You will learn how to move database icons around workspace pages, change color and pattern settings, manage the workspace and other open Notes windows, and manage the size of your workspace. The workspace is also a good place to begin navigating around in Notes.

Once you have mastered the Notes workspace, the next chapter will lead you through finding and opening Notes databases, show you how add databases to your workspace, and open, close, and find databases on your workspace, your hard drive, and Notes servers.

A Map of the Workspace

Here is a map of the Notes workspace to guide you to the various parts and controls. By default, the workspace is made up of six tabbed pages. The Replicator page is always the last tab in the workspace and is used for scheduling and initiating database replication, covered in detail in Chapter 14, "Using the Notes Replicator."

TIP SHEET

▶ **To customize your SmartIcon settings, choose File, Tools, SmartIcons. The SmartIcons dialog box appears with options to move the position of the bar, edit icons, hide the bar, and make SmartIcons context-sensitive.**

▶ **On the Notes workspace for the Macintosh, the menu bar is at the top of the screen, the SmartIcons are below the menu bar, and the title bar of the active window is below the SmartIcons.**

▶ **To view both the file name and the server name of a database on the database's icon, hold down the Shift key while you choose View, Show Server Names. The file name includes the entire path (a string of directories or folders) of the file.**

▶ **Stacking replica database icons helps you organize your workspace even further. You have the option of accessing the same database from a number of different locations, which comes in handy when an individual Notes server is not currently accessible, or if another replica has more up-to-date information. To stack replica database icons, make the Notes workspace the active window and choose View, Stack Replica Icons. To undo a stacking, deselect the View, Stack Replica Icons selection from the menu.**

▶ **To display unread counts on database icons, make the workspace the active window and choose View, Show Unread. To update unread counts choose View, Refresh Unread Count (or press F9).**

Lotus Notes - Workspace at Travel

▶ **1** The title bar indicates the name of the active window.

Max Martin's Mail on Local

7 The down arrow in the upper-right corner indicates that the database icon is a stack of replicas. A replica is an identical copy of a database residing in another location (usually another Notes server). The current replica is the icon on the top.

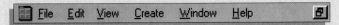

2 The menu bar provides the menu action items you can select from. The menu actions change depending on the current window.

3 The SmartIcon bar offers a number of common Notes actions you perform on a regular basis, such as opening a new database and saving a file. You can learn what a SmartIcon's function is by holding the pointer over the SmartIcon (on the Macintosh you first need to turn on Balloon Help).

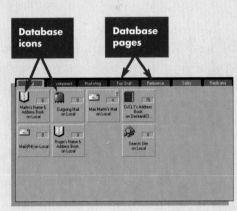

Database icons

Database pages

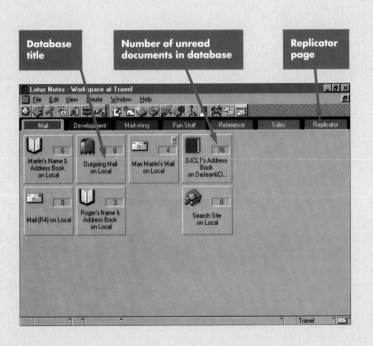

Database title

Number of unread documents in database

Replicator page

4 The entire workspace contains by default six pages (plus the Replicator page), each with the database icons you have added to it. Each page is identified by a colored tab with a descriptive name.

Where database is located

6 "Local" indicates that the database resides on a local drive (your hard drive); a server name would indicate that the database resides on a Notes server.

5 Double-click on a database icon to open the actual database.

A Map of the Status Bar

The status bar is the along the bottom of the Notes workspace. The options are listed in pop-up menus. Click on any one of these options to display the pop-up menu of options. You can use these options to determine when Notes is accessing a Notes server (a lightening bolt appears on the network or a modem icon appears for remote users). You can also use these options to change the font, size, and style of text, see a list of recent messages from Notes, see your level of access to the current database, see your current location and edit it, and use the pop-up mail menu to create and read mail.

► **1** The status bar's leftmost box tells you when you are accessing the network (with a lightening bolt), or connected to a Notes server by way of a modem (with a modem simulating flashing red and green LED lights when data is transferred).

8 Click on the rightmost box to display a pop-up menu of mail options and tasks to perform, such as creating a new mail memo, scanning mail, sending mail, and opening mail.

7 The location box indicates your current location and allows you to switch between locations or edit a Location document. For more details on Locations, see Chapter 13, Using Mobile Notes.

- ▸ You can switch between locations by selecting a location from the location pop-up menu.

- ▸ You must have the cursor in a rich text field to change the font, style, or size of text.

- ▸ The status bar is always at the bottom of your Notes workspace and/or the active Notes window. Under Windows 95 the status bar appears above the Windows 95 task bar, unless you have moved it.

2 Use the Font box to change the typeface of rich text you are editing.

3 Use the Font Size box to to change the size of rich text you are editing.

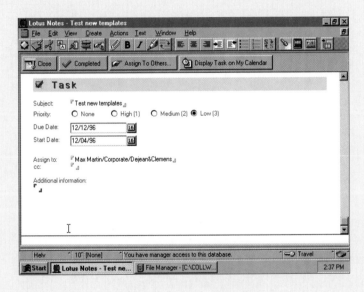

4 The Style box lets you change the style of rich text you are editing.

6 The next box tells you the level of access you have to the database you are currently viewing. For more details on database access, see Chapter 5, "Using Notes Databases."

5 The command history box gives you a list of the most recent actions carried out in Notes.

How to Manage Your Workspace Pages

Now that you are familiar with the Notes workspace, this page shows you how to manage the workspace and its pages to best suit your needs.

Notes stores the information about your workspace in a file called DESKTOP.DSK. This file is found in your Notes Data directory (or the Data folder on the Macintosh). The DESK-TOP.DSK file remembers the database icons you add to the workspace pages, the number of documents unread in each database, and private views and folders you add to databases.

TIP SHEET

▶ **It is a good idea to make a backup of your DESKTOP.DSK file once you have added a substantial number of databases. Otherwise, if for some reason the file is corrupted or deleted, you would have to add all those databases from scratch, which can be time consuming.**

▶ **If your DESKTOP.DSK file is from an older version of Notes, you will be asked if you want to upgrade your workspace (DESKTOP.DSK file). Once you add a workspace page to your desktop it is converted to a new desktop file and can no longer be used with older versions of Notes.**

▶ **Under Windows, OS/2, and UNIX you can keep the workspace in the back of all other open windows. Then every time you close a window, Notes will go to the next current window, instead of the workspace. To do this, choose File, Tools, User Preferences and under Advanced Options select the Keep Workspace In Back When Maximized option.**

1 This is the current workspace page. To switch to another workspace page, select the page's tab with the mouse pointer. To switch to another page with the keyboard, press the Ctrl key (or the Command key on the Macintosh) and then the left or right arrow key.

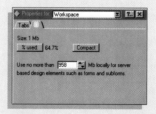

6 You can reduce the amount of disk space taken up by your workspace files (DESKTOP.DSK and CACHE.DSK files) by compacting these files. To do this, double-click on one of the workspace page tabs. In the Properties box, select the Information tab (the i) and then select the %Used button to see how much free, unused space there is in the workspace files. Select the Compact button if the percentage of used space is under 85%. You can keep the CACHE.DSK file (one of the two workspace files) from growing large by setting the maximum size (in megabytes; Mb) it can grow to in the Use No More Than _ Mb Locally For Server Based Design Elements Such As Forms And Subforms box.

2 To create a new workspace page, make the workspace the active window and choose Create, Workspace Page. Notes inserts the new page to the left of the currently selected page. You can have up to 32 workspace pages.

3 You can delete a workspace page by selecting the workspace's tab and choosing Edit, Clear. Be sure that you want to do this operation—when you delete the workspace page, Notes removes all the database icons contained on that page from your Notes workspace.

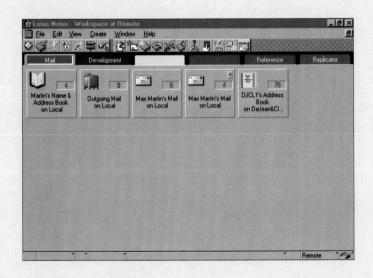

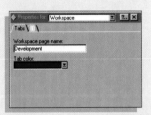

4 To enter or change a name of a workspace page tab, or change the tab's color, double-click on the workspace page tab and the Properties box for the workspace appears. You can enter a name up to 32 characters long and choose from a large palette of colors by holding down the arrow button.

5 You can display your workspace in 3-D (three-dimensions) by choosing File, Tools, User Preferences, and then selecting the Textured Workspace option under Advanced Options. Under Windows, OS/2, and UNIX you can display your workspace in monochrome (shades of gray instead of colors) by selecting the Monochrome Display option under Advanced Options.

CHAPTER 4

Adding Notes Databases to Your Workspace

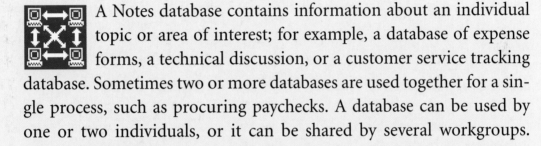 A Notes database contains information about an individual topic or area of interest; for example, a database of expense forms, a technical discussion, or a customer service tracking database. Sometimes two or more databases are used together for a single process, such as procuring paychecks. A database can be used by one or two individuals, or it can be shared by several workgroups. Notes databases stored on a Notes server are shared by many Notes users, while a database stored on your local drive is used only by you.

The information in a database is stored in documents. Each document can contain text, graphics, interactive objects (such as hotspots and buttons), and other types of information. In general, as you add more documents to a database, it grows in size.

To access a database, you must first find the location of the database, either on a Notes server, your local drive, or a network drive, and then add the database icon to the workspace and open it. Once the database icon is on your workspace, you can simply double-click on the icon to open the database.

This chapter will teach you how to add databases to your workspace and open them, and how to find databases on your local drive and on a Notes server. Then the next chapter will dive into teaching you how to open databases once they are on your workspace, how to move database icons around the workspace, how to get information about a database, and how to find database replicas.

How to Add a Database from a Notes Server

There are several ways to add a database to your workspace. You can find and add a database from a Notes server, add a database from your local hard drive, add a database from a network drive, add a database by typing in the database's file name, or browse a library of available databases and add them directly to your workspace. This page shows you how to add a database to your workspace when it resides on a Notes server.

▶ **The Open Database dialog box shows only servers that you have previously added databases from. In order to see all the servers in your Notes domain, select the Other option at the bottom of the list of servers (from the Server option). Your Notes administrator(s) will create one or more Notes domains, and you can see all the Notes servers in your domain in the Choose Other Server dialog box.**

▶ **When you are connected remotely (as a mobile user), you can select a database from a server on a network through the Open Database dialog box simply by selecting the server. A dialog box will then appear asking you if you want to dial the server now.**

▶ **When you remove a database icon while the database is still open, the icon will remain on your workspace until the database is closed.**

▶ **To find which Notes server(s) a database resides on, use a Database Catalog (the file name is CATALOG.NSF) found on a Notes server you have access to. A Notes administrator must set up the Database Catalog, so if you cannot find it, ask the Notes administrator where it is, or where the database you are trying to find is located.**

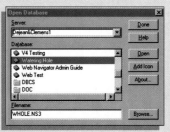

1 When you know which server a database is located on, choose File, Database, Open. You can now select a database from the server currently showing (which is Local by default), or choose a different server to view using the Server option.

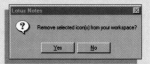

7 To remove a database icon from your workspace, select the database icon and choose Edit, Clear or press the Del (delete) key. Select Yes in the dialog box that asks you if you want to remove the selected icon(s) from your workspace. To select more than one icon, select one icon and then hold down the Shift key while you select the remaining icons. On Windows, OS/2, and UNIX you can click the right mouse button and choose Remove From Workspace.

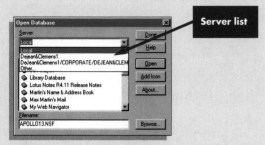

Server list

2 To find a Notes server that is not listed in the pop-up list of servers, choose Other at the bottom of the list.

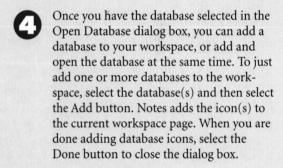

3 The Choose Other Server dialog box appears with an alternative list of servers. Select a server and then select the OK button.

4 Once you have the database selected in the Open Database dialog box, you can add a database to your workspace, or add and open the database at the same time. To just add one or more databases to the workspace, select the database(s) and then select the Add button. Notes adds the icon(s) to the current workspace page. When you are done adding database icons, select the Done button to close the dialog box.

5 You will notice when you select the database that the database's file name appears at the bottom of the Open Database dialog box. The database's title is listed in the list of databases.

6 To add the icon and open the database, select the database and then select the Open button. As soon as you select the Open button, Notes will close the dialog box, add the icon to your workspace (to the current workspace page), and open the database.

How to Add a Database from Your Local Drive

You can add a database stored locally on your hard drive (or any local or network drive) to your workspace. When Local is chosen as the server in the Open Database dialog box, the databases listed in your Notes Data directory (Data folder on the Macintosh) have .NSF file extensions. You also see any subdirectories in the data directory. You can add databases stored inside and outside of your data directory to your workspace.

► **1** Choose File, Database, Open to open the Open Database dialog box.

10 Click on the Add button to add the database icon to your workspace. You can keep adding database icons to the workspace from this dialog box. When you are finished adding icons, select the Done button to close the dialog box.

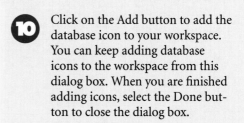

9 When you find the database you want, select it and click on the Select button. Notes brings you back to the Open Database dialog box, and inserts the full path of the database you have selected in the Filename text box.

2 Select the database you want to open from the list of databases. The Local directory (your data directory) is shown by default.

3 If the database you want to open is in a subdirectory (or folder) inside the data directory, open that subdirectory by double-clicking on it (or select the subdirectory and then select the Open button).

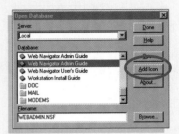

4 You can add a database's icon to your workspace, or add the icon and open the database at the same time. To add a database to your workspace, select the database and then select the Add Icon button. Continue this process of adding databases until you are done, then select the Done button to close the Open Database dialog box.

5 You will notice when you select the database, the database's file name appears at the bottom of the Open Database dialog. The database's title is listed in the list of databases.

6 To add a database and open it at the same time, select the database from the list of databases and then select the Open button. Notes will close the Open Database dialog box, add the database icon to your workspace, and then open the database.

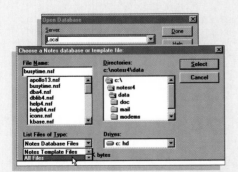

8 By default, this dialog box displays only Notes database files when it is first opened; however, you can display just Notes template files, or all files. See the Tip Sheet on this page for more details on Notes template and database files.

7 To open a database stored outside the Notes Data directory (local drive), choose File, Open, Database. In the Open Database dialog box, select the Browse button. A dialog box appears asking you to choose a database or template file. You can now navigate throughout your drive(s) to select a database to add to your workspace. For example, if you have a database on a CD-ROM or network drive, select the drive from the list of drives under the Drives option.

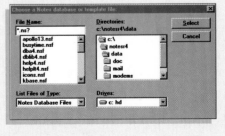

How to Add a Database Using a File Name

When you know the file name of a database, you can type in the full path name of the database in the Open Database dialog box to either add the database to your workspace, or both add the icon and open the database.

▶ **1** Choose File, Database, Open to bring up the Open Database dialog box.

▸ **Each Notes client platform (Windows, OS/2, Macintosh, and UNIX) supports a slightly different style for designating a file's path, so take this into consideration when you enter file names into the Open Database dialog box. For example, the Macintosh uses colons (:) to separate folders (directories), and can have spaces between characters, as in the path PPC HD:Lotus Notes:Data:names.nsf.**

▸ **In UNIX, the directory and file names are case-sensitive, (and directories are separated by backward slashes), so REPORTS\REPORTS97.NSF is not the same as Reports\Reports97.NSF.**

6 In some cases, the Notes administrator may designate special databases to appear in a special dialog box, in order to add them to your workspace quickly. To add databases with this designation, choose File, Database, Open Special. Speak to your Notes administrator for more information on special databases.

2 Place the cursor (click in) the Filename text box and type in the full path name of the database file you want to add and/or open. For example, a database with the file name REPORTS97.NSF is in a subdirectory called REPORTS in your Data directory. You would enter REPORTS\ REPORTS97.NSF into the Filename text box.

3 Once you have entered the file name, select the Open button to open the database, or select the Add button to add the database to your workspace.

4 Alternatively, you can enter a database file name for a database that resides on a Notes server. For example, to open a database with the file name Projects97.NSF, which resides on a server called Marketing2, you would type Marketing2!!Projects97.NSF in the Filename text box, and then select the Open button.

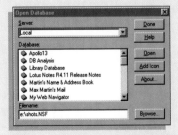

5 To open a database stored on a local drive outside the Notes data directory, enter the path name in the Filename text box. For example, a database with the file name shots.NSF is stored on the E drive. So the full path entered into the dialog box would be e:\shots.NSF.

CHAPTER 5

Using and Managing Notes Databases

This chapter will show you how to manage your day-to-day use of Notes databases. In the course of using Notes, you may want to move some database icons around to different workspace pages, open multiple databases simultaneously, delete a database from a server or local hard drive, or find more information about a specific database.

Also covered here are database *replicas*. A replica is an identical copy of a database, which can replicate (exchange) data with another replica copy of the database in order to keep the replica copies in sync. Databases almost always have replicas of each other, with each database replica existing on a separate Notes server. In some cases, such as your mail file, a replica is stored on your local drive. This chapter shows you how to locate replica copies of a database on your workspace.

In addition, you may need information about a database to determine how to use it. Every database has information and help documents that can assist you in using the database, and this is discussed in this chapter as well.

Finally, you will learn about database access and how it affects your database use. Notes databases have various levels of access to maintain data security and the integrity of the database design. This is accomplished with a series of roles and levels that each user is assigned. A database administrator determines and manages Notes users' individual access to databases. Herein we'll show you how to view your access level to a database, and discuss what the different access levels are.

How to Move Database Icons Around and Open Them

You can move database icons around workspace pages to suit the way you work. For example, you may want all your mail-related databases on one workspace page, and your marketing-related databases on another workspace page. Here are some techniques for moving icons around, opening databases by using icons, and deleting icons and databases. Make sure to read the section on how to find and open replica databases using icons later in this chapter.

▶❶ Database icons can be placed anywhere on an individual workspace page. To move a database icon around a workspace page, select and drag it with your mouse cursor. Notice that the cursor turns into a hand, and that a hollow rectangle moves with the hand as you drag the icon. The rectangle represents the database icon you are moving. Once you have dragged the icon to its new location, let go of the mouse button.

❼ You can also neatly arrange all the icons on an individual workspace page in rows. To do this, make the workspace the active window and select the tab for the page you want to arrange. Choose View, Arrange Icons.

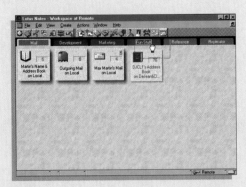

2 To move a database icon from one workspace page to another, drag the icon (using the mouse cursor) over the tab of the workspace page you want to move the icon to. When the icon is over the workspace page tab (you will see the tab name outlined) release the icon (let go of the mouse button) and the icon will have moved to the new workspace page.

3 To open a database icon from the workspace, double-click on the icon.

4 You can also open a database by selecting a database icon and then pressing the Enter key, or by selecting the database icon and choosing File, Open.

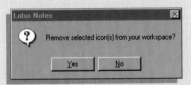

5 To remove an icon from a workspace page, select the icon and press the Del key (del key on the Macintosh). Click on Yes when the dialog box appears asking you if you want to remove the icon.

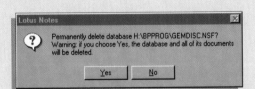

6 You can delete a database from not only your workspace, but also from the server or local drive the database resides on. Be aware that this action is *not* reversible—by deleting the database you will no longer have the database and will not be able to add it to your workspace again. You will have to retrieve a backup copy of the database (if you have made one), or obtain a replica copy of the database (if there is a replica available on another Notes server). To delete a database, select the database icon and choose File, Database, Delete. Click on the Yes button in the dialog box asking you if you want to permanently delete the database.

How to Open Two or More Databases at a Time

You can open one database at a time, or two or more databases at the same time. This is useful when you want to view the contents of more than one database without having to switch between different database windows. The active window will contain a view of each database's folder, views, and documents. In addition, if you are using Windows 95 you can create a shortcut for opening a Notes database directly from the Windows 95 desktop. If you are using a Macintosh you can use a shortcut for opening a Notes database from the Mac OS Finder.

▶ **1** To open two or more databases, hold down the Shift key (shift key on the Macintosh) and select each database you want to open. Then either double-click on one of the selected icons or press the Enter key (return key on the Macintosh). Note that you can select multiple database icons on different workspace pages simply by switching between workspace page tabs. As long as you continue to hold down the Shift key as you select icons, they will all remain selected.

8 If you use the Macintosh, you can open a database from the Macintosh Finder. Go to the Finder and drag the database file icon over the Notes program icon. Notes will open (if it not already) and then open the database to the default view.

7 Now drag a database icon you want to create the shortcut for out to the desktop. The shortcut is now on your Windows 95 desktop. When you use the shortcut, Notes will open the database to the default view.

TIP SHEET

▶ **When you cannot find a database icon that you believe is somewhere on your workspace, you can try to add or open the database again by choosing File, Database, Open. If the icon is on your workspace, Notes will tell you it has already been added and will then give you the chance to open it again when you select the Open button from the Open Database dialog box. Notes will also highlight the database icon (on the workspace) you are trying to find and open.**

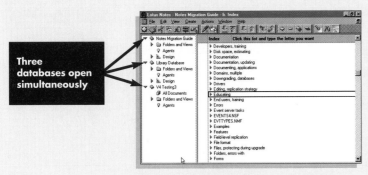

Three databases open simultaneously

2 In this example, three databases were selected on the workspace. The three database titles appear in the navigation pane on the left.

3 You can expand each of the database folders and views as well as switch to each database to view the contents of their folders and views.

4 Keep in mind that you do not have to open two or more databases simultaneously to view them in the same active window. You can open each individually by selecting each one at a time and then double-clicking on the icons to open the databases in their own window.

5 You can choose to Tile, Cascade, Minimize All, or Maximize All your open Notes windows by choosing one of the options under the Window menu. In addition, you can switch between open windows by choosing a window listed on the second half of the Window menu.

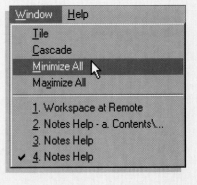

6 If you use Windows 95, you can open a Notes database from the Windows 95 desktop by creating a shortcut. First, resize the Notes window (by selecting the window resizing icon) so you can see the Windows 95 desktop.

How to Find a Replica of a Database

Most often there is more than one copy of a Notes database available to you. Notes allows you to store multiple copies of a single database on multiple servers and/or workstations. These identical copies are called replicas. One replica copy resides on each individual server and/or workstation. Then, when a database is modified, replica copies can *replicate* with each other to exchange information, keeping each other in sync. This allows you to access a database from a number of possible servers you have access to, as well as from your local drive when you want to open the database locally.

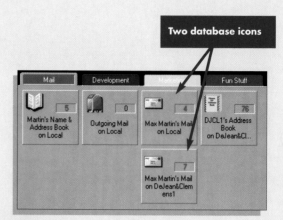

1 Here are two database icons representing replicas of the same database, Max Martin's mail. One replica is on a local drive and the other is on a server.

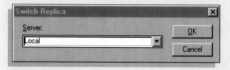

9 You can also switch between replicas when database icons are not stacked (and may be hard to find). This will change the replica icon associated with the current database icon and point to a different replica in a different location (on a different server). To do this, select a database icon for which you want to switch replicas. Choose File, Replication, Switch Replica, and then in the Switch Replica dialog box select the server (or local drive) to switch the icon to.

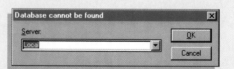

8 You may encounter an instance where Notes cannot find the database you are trying to open. It is possible that the Notes administrator has moved the database to another directory or another Notes server, so check with your Notes administrator about relocated databases. If you receive the Database Cannot Be Found dialog box, you can try to search other servers for the database by selecting another server the database might be found on.

2 To stack the replica icons, select View, Stack Replica Icons. Now the icons are stacked on top of one another.

3 The icon on the top of the stack is the replica that will open when the database icon is double-clicked. To open another replica of the same database, click on and hold down the arrow button to reveal the list of replicas stacked on the database icon.

4 When you select a replica on another server (or local drive) from the menu of replicas, that replica becomes the top icon on the stack. You can now double-click the icon to open the replica.

5 You can find another replica for a database icon already added to your workspace. This allows you to search for other Notes servers that may have a replica of the database. This is useful when you are not able to connect with a particular server, and would like to find another server that contains a replica of the database. To find a replica, select the database icon (or have the database open) and choose File, Replication, Find Replica.

7 For more on how to replicate a database and create your own replica copies, see Chapter 13, "Using Mobile Notes."

6 The Add Replica To Workspace dialog box appears. Select a server from the Server menu or select Other to find another server to search for a replica of the database. You can also type the name of the server in this dialog box.

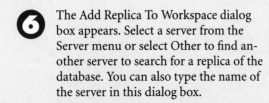

How to Find Information about a Database

You can find information about a database at any time: before you add it to your workspace, after you have added it, or while you are using it. In addition, Help documents specific to each database are available to you, as are general database properties for every database. You can also view the level of access you have to a database. Notes databases have different levels of access to maintain data security and the integrity of the database design.

TIP SHEET

▸ Here is a brief definition of each of the access level in a database ACL (Access Control List): No Access = Users cannot access the database; Depositor = Users can create documents but cannot see any documents; Reader = Users can read documents, but cannot create or edit documents; Author = Users can create documents and edit only the documents they create; Editor = Users can create documents, and edit all documents (those created by others as well as their own); Designer = Users can modify the database design, modify replication formulas, create a full text index, and perform all tasks allowed by lower access levels; Manager = Users can modify the ACL, encrypt a database for local security, modify replication settings, delete special tasks, and perform tasks allowed by all other access levels. Within each access level individual rights can be granted and revoked by the Manager. These rights are listed under Access, and become active as different access levels are chosen.

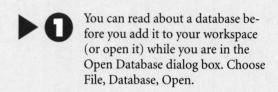

1 You can read about a database before you add it to your workspace (or open it) while you are in the Open Database dialog box. Choose File, Database, Open.

7 To see more general information about a database, open the Properties infobox for the database. To do this, select the database icon or open the database, and choose File, Database, Properties. The Basics tab contains the database title, the location of the database, the file name, and other miscellaneous information. Additional tabs contain information about the size of the database, its design settings, printing settings, and full text index.

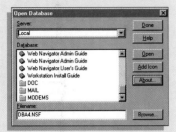

2 Select the database in the list of databases and then select the About button.

3 The About Database document is displayed for you to read. When you are finished reading it, select the Close button and you will be back in the Open Database dialog box.

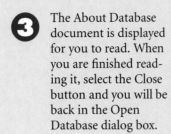

4 To find help on using a database already added to your workspace, select the database on the workspace (or have it open and make it the active window) and then choose Help, Using This Database. To view the About Database document for a database, select the database icon (or have it open and make it the active window) and choose Help, About This Database.

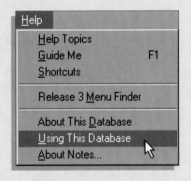

6 The levels of access include: Manager, Designer, Editor, Author, Reader, Depositor, and No Access. Access levels are assigned to users (and group names) to control what they can do in a database. Most users of a database located on a server have Author access, which means they can both create documents in the database and edit the documents they create. For a full description of what each access level allows, see the Tip Sheet on this page.

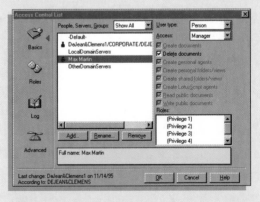

5 To view the level of access you have to a database, select or open the database and choose File, Database, Access Control. This is the database's Access Control List (ACL).

TRY IT!

You have now acquired the skills both to navigate around your Notes workspace and add Notes databases to workspace pages. Here is your chance to test your mastery of Notes this far.

We will create a new workspace page, and add a database to the new page by both dragging a database icon from another workspace page and adding a database from a Notes server. Some steps have notation referring to the chapter where the step was covered.

Make your Notes workspace the active window. If you are in another window, choose the workspace window from the Window menu. *Chapter 3*

Now add a new Workspace Page tab to your workspace. Remember to select a Workspace Page tab directly to the right of the position where you want the new tab to appear. For example, to create the new workspace page before the Replicator page, select the Replicator tab. *Chapter 3*

 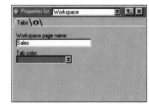

Assign a name to your new Workspace Page tab. Select a color for the tab as well *Chapter 3*

Close the Properties box for the new workspace page.

Go to the tab that contains your Personal Name and Address Book.

Move the database icon for your Personal Name and Address Book to the new workspace page. *Chapter 5*

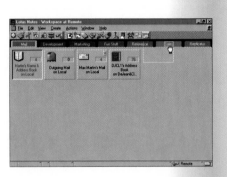

Now you are going to add a database from a server to the new workspace page. Open the Open Database dialog box. *Chapters 4 and 5*

Select a server from which you can view a list of databases. *Chapter 4*

If you are not currently connected to a server, select a server and Notes will dial the server for you. *Chapter 4*

Select a database and add it to your workspace. *Chapter 4*

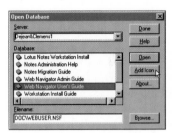

Now move your Personal Name and Address Book icon back to the workspace page it was previously on. *Chapter 3*

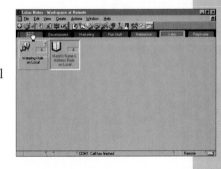

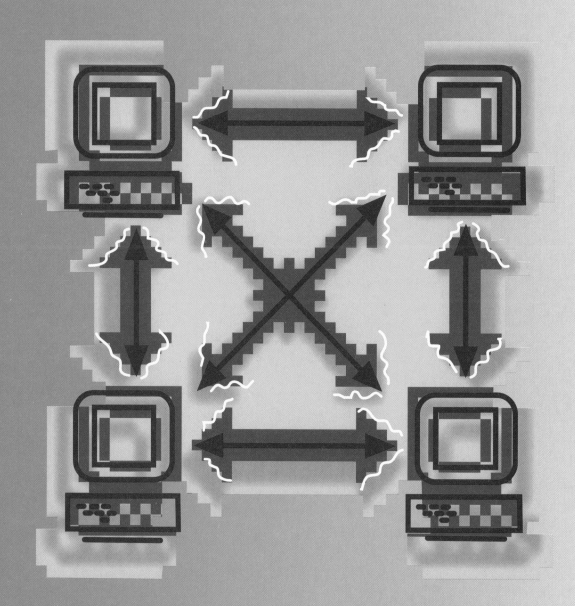

CHAPTER 6

Notes Panes and Views

 A Notes database opens up to three panes: the navigation pane, the view pane, and the preview pane. One pane is always the selected or active pane.

The first time you open a database the default view of the database is opened. You can then switch to other views in the database. When you close the database and then open it again later, the database will open to the view you were last in.

This chapter shows you how to use and take advantage of these three panes, and how to manage views and documents in a database. The next chapter shows you how to manage folders, which reside in the navigation pane and are similar to views in many ways.

An Introduction to Database View

There are three panes that make up database view—navigation, view, and preview—and all are discussed in detail here and in the following pages of this chapter.

1 The navigation pane displays the views, folders (shared and private), agents, and design elements that make up a database when the database design allows it to be shown.

8 Documents in the view pane are marked with an asterisk (*) when they are new and/or have not been read yet. The document titles may also appear in red until they have been read or marked read.

7 The view may also display the search bar. This is used to search for documents that meet a certain search query or criteria. Searching databases is discussed in detail in Chapter 16.

TIP SHEET

▸ To jump between the three panes, press the F6 key.

▸ To navigate up or down within a document when the preview pane is active, use the up or down arrow keys on your keyboard.

▸ To navigate through a document while still in the view pane, hold down the Alt key while pressing the up or down arrow keys. When you let go of the Alt key (option key on the Macintosh), the view pane becomes the active pane again. The Alt key and the Page Up or Page Down keys (page up and page down on a Macintosh extended keyboard) also allow you to scroll in a document, page by page.

2 In some cases, the navigation pane displays navigators (interactive graphics) instead of the usual list of views, folders, and agents. When you select a navigator graphic, it performs an action such as opening another view or another navigator.

3 The view pane displays some or all of the documents stored in the database. You can double-click on a document to open it from the view pane. The view pane displays document information in columns; there is one column for each type of information for a document. Categories appear in rows; there is one row for each category, or a single (or multiline) document title and accompanying information.

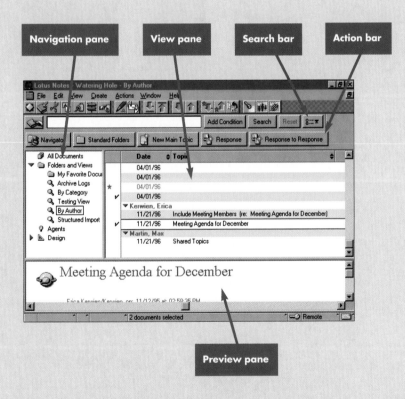

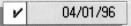

4 You can select one or more documents by placing a checkmark next to the document in the left-most column in the view pane.

5 The preview pane displays the document currently highlighted in the view pane. The preview pane allows you to read the contents of the document as well as edit it.

6 A database view can also have an action bar which contains one or more buttons. A button, when selected (clicked with the mouse), performs common shortcuts and tasks specific to the current view.

How to Manage Database Panes

You can adjust the panes in a database based on how you want to view the database information. All three panes are resizeable and can be reorganized and/or hidden. This page shows you how to adjust the panes and also shows you how to use the navigation pane and navigators.

▶ **1** You can change the size of any pane, making it larger or smaller, narrower or wider. When you change one pane, the sizes of the other panes adjust to fit the window size.

8 Expand the list of folders and views in the navigation pane. The folder icon represents a folder, and the magnifying glass icon represents a view. Select a folder or view and it becomes the active folder (or view) in the view pane.

7 The navigation pane lists the views and folders to choose from. Select the All Documents view to view all the documents in the database.

TIP SHEET

▶ **The light bulb icon in the navigation pane represents the database's agents. When you select the agent icon (the light bulb) the database's agent(s) appear in the view pane. For more details about agents and how to create an agent, see Chapter 17, "Creating Agents."**

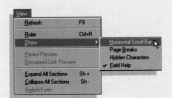

2 To adjust the panes, move the cursor over the edge of the pane you are resizing. You can drag the edge horizontally or vertically once you see the black line with two arrows appear.

3 You can hide (or show) the preview pane by choosing View, Document Preview. A checkmark next to the menu option means the option is turned on.

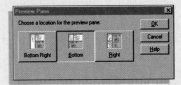

4 You can arrange the overall layout of the three panes with regard to the preview pane by choosing View, Arrange Preview. Select the icon that represents where you want the preview pane to appear: on the bottom right, bottom, or right side of the window.

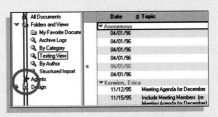

6 When the preview pane is the active pane, you can adjust settings for it. Choose View, Show, Horizontal Scroll Bar to add a horizontal scroll bar to the preview pane. Now you can scroll across a document to view its hidden parts.

5 You can hide or display a pane by dragging the outer edge of a pane. For example, to hide the navigation pane, drag the right edge all the way to the left. To display the navigation pane again, drag the left edge over toward the right. You can drag the other panes closed or open in this way as well.

How to Manage Documents in a View

There are a number of ways to view documents in a database. The preview pane allows you to view each document while still viewing all the documents in a particular view. Here are some ways to manage, read, and edit documents in a view.

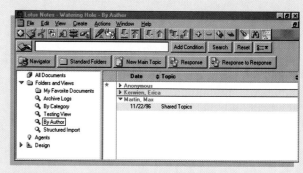

▶ **1** You can expand or collapse a main document or a category in a view by selecting the arrow next to it.

10 To edit the document in the preview pane, double-click on the document in the preview pane. To open the document in its own window, double-click on the document in the view pane.

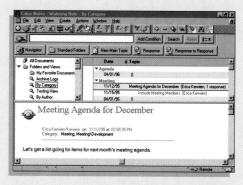

9 You can read a document provided that the preview pane is open. Select the document in the view pane. The contents of the document now appear in the preview pane.

TIP SHEET

▶ You can select one or more documents in a view at the same time. Selected documents have a checkmark next to them. When one document is highlighted (with or without a checkmark next to it) it is considered the selected document. To select two or more documents, drag the cursor up or down the left-most column (gutter) until checkmarks appear next to the documents. To select or deselect the documents in a view choose Edit, Select All or Edit, Deselect All.

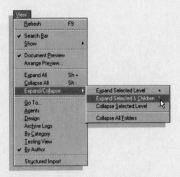

2 You can expand or collapse a main document, category, or the entire view using menu options. To expand or collapse all the documents in the current view, choose View, Expand All, or View, Collapse All.

3 To expand or collapse only a selected level of the documents, use the menu options next to View, Expand/Collapse. This menu also allows you to collapse all folders in the navigation pane by choosing View, Expand/Collapse, Collapse All Folders.

4 You can refresh a view to see new documents that have been added to the database since you first opened the view and began using the database. This can happen if a database has replicated with another replica, or other users are adding, editing, or deleting documents in the database while you are working in the database (when the database resides on a server). This is also useful when you want to see new mail that has arrived while you are working in your mail database.

5 To refresh a view, make the view pane active and choose View, Refresh (or press F9). You can also tell if a view needs to be refreshed if this icon appears in the top left corner of the view pane. Click on the icon to refresh the view.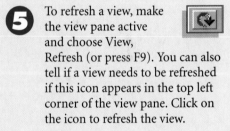

6 To switch to another view, select the view in the navigation pane. You may have to expand the Folders and Views icon to see the views to choose from.

8 You can select documents to categorize or delete in batch mode. To select documents, click next to the document in the left-most column (gutter) in the view pane. A checkmark appears next to a selected document. You can now view only selected documents by choosing View, Show, Selected Only. To undo the command and see all the documents in the view again, choose View, Show, Selected Only again to remove the checkmark next to the menu option.

7 To view only documents that you haven't opened or marked as read yet, open the view and choose View, Show, Unread Only. To undo the command and see all the documents in the view again, choose View, Show, Unread again to remove the checkmark next to the menu option.

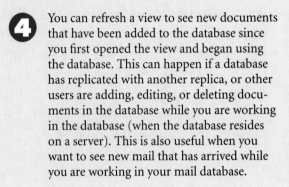

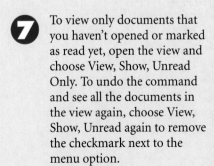

How to Manage Categorized Views

Views can be designed (by the database's designer) to be categorized. Categories in a view organize documents so you can understand how documents in a view are related to one another. Categories may be sorted (this is determined by the database designer) so that they appear alphabetically or numerically in ascending or descending order (this is also determined by the database designer).

▶ ❶ To categorize documents, select the documents by placing checkmarks next to them. Then choose Actions, Categorize.

❿ To delete a category you must first remove all the documents from it (select the documents, and then deselect the category in the Categorize dialog box and click on OK). Once the database is closed and opened again, the category will no longer appear in the view and the documents will be listed as Not Categorized. Alternatively, you can select another category to avoid having the documents under Not Categorized.

❾ To rename a category you must recategorize all documents under a new category (the old category will disappear). Select all the documents under the category you want to change and choose Actions, Categorize. Select the existing category in the list of category names to remove the checkmark (deselect it). Now type in the new category name in the New Categories text box and select the OK button.

❽ To uncategorize documents, select the documents and choose Actions, Categorize. Deselect the category or categories to remove the checkmark next to the category, then select the OK button.

TIP SHEET

▶ **You can have up to 32 category levels. Enter additional levels of subcategories using the backslash technique, as described in step 6 on this page.**

▶ **You can use a subcategory twice for the same document by entering each category followed by a comma in the Categorize dialog box. For example: Meeting\Development, Meeting\Sales.**

▶ **You can display only categories in a view by choosing View, Show, Categories Only.**

2 The Categorize dialog box asks you to choose one or more categories to list the documents under. For a category to exist in a view it must have at least one document in it.

3 You can add one or more category names in the text box at the bottom. To create two or more categories, type each category name in, separated by commas. For example, **Sales, Marketing, Development.**

4 Subcategories appear indented from main categories (or parent categories), but they do not appear in the Categorize dialog box (when you choose Actions, Categorize). To create a subcategory, place a checkmark next to each document you want to categorize and choose Actions, Categorize.

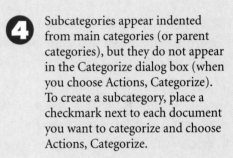

5 Enter the category name followed by a backslash (\) and the subcategory name in the New Categories text box. For example, **Meeting\Development** indicates the category is Meeting and the subcategory is Development. Select OK to close the dialog box and subcategorize the selected documents.

6 Now the selected documents are subcategorized, as in this example.

7 To place documents into an already existing subcategory, first select the documents you want to subcategorize. Now choose Actions, Categorize, and type in the name of the category followed by a backslash (\) and the subcategory name, with the exact spelling.

How to Copy, Paste, and Delete Documents in a View

You can manage and move documents around in a view using the Notes copy, paste, and delete features within a view. This page shows you how to do this. Keep in mind that views are designed to show all or part of the documents the database is storing, which means the view is limited to displaying only the documents it is designed to display.

As with categorizing documents, you must select a document or group of documents to act on them, whether you are copying them, deleting them, categorizing them, or printing them.

1 To copy a document, select the document in the view and choose Edit, Copy. You can copy one or more documents by selecting them in the view.

TIP SHEET

▸ **In most cases you should make sure you are pasting documents into a database that contains the form the document can be read with. The easiest way to ensure this is to copy and paste documents between databases with similar or identical designs. When you paste a document into a database that does not have the appropriate form to view the document, the database uses its default form to display it. The problem here is that the default form may not have all the appropriate fields to display the contents of the document.**

▸ **You need at least Author access to the database to delete documents you have created. You need Editor access to delete documents others have created.**

2 Once you have copied a document, you can paste it into another database. Open the database you want copy the document(s) to and choose Edit, Paste.

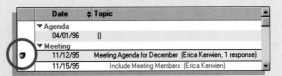

3 To delete one or more documents you must first mark (or select) them for deletion. Documents marked for deletion have a trash can icon next to them in the left-most column in the view pane.

4 To mark a document for deletion, select the document(s) you want to delete and choose Edit, Clear. A selected document can also be marked for deletion by pressing the Delete key (del key on the Macintosh).

5 To remove the delete mark (the trash can icon) from the documents, select them and choose Edit, Undo Delete. Alternatively, you can select the document marked for deletion and then press the Delete key to toggle the trash can icon on and off.

6 To delete the documents from the database, either close the documents, or refresh the database view by pressing F9 or choosing View, Refresh. Be sure that you want to delete them because this step is not reversible! Depending on how you have set your Empty Trash Folder option in User Preferences, you may be prompted to confirm that you want to delete these documents permanently.

CHAPTER 7

Notes Folders

 Folders appear in the navigation pane of a database, and they allow you to manage documents without having to categorize them in a particular view.

There are two types of folders: personal and shared. Personal folders are the folders you create in a database, and shared folders are used and shared by other users of the database. You alone have access to your personal folder; however, you must have at least Reader access to the database to create a personal folder. To create a shared folder you must have at least Editor access to the database and the Create Shared Folders/Views option must be selected in the database's ACL (Access Control List).

A personal folder is stored either in the database or in your DESKTOP.DSK file, and where it is stored is determined by the manager of the database (as a setting in the database's ACL). When the Create Shared Folders/Views option is selected in the database's ACL, you can store personal folders in the database. Otherwise, personal folders are stored in your DESKTOP.DSK file.

In this chapter we'll show you how to create and manage personal folders. Keep in mind that you can only use personal folders from your workstation when your folders are stored in the DESKTOP.DSK file.

How to Create a Personal Folder

A folder is created primarily for organization, and when the views in a database do not organize and/or display documents as you would like.

You can copy a folder from another database or create a folder from scratch. Here's how to do both.

▶ **1** To copy a folder from a database that is similar to the kind you want, open the database, select the navigation pane, and choose Create, Folder.

2 Give the folder a name and select the Options button. In the Options dialog box select Blank and click on the OK button.

3 To create a folder from scratch, select the database and choose Create, Folder.

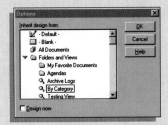

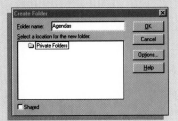

2 Enter a name for the folder in the Folder Name text box.

3 Select the Options button to open the Options dialog box. You can now select a design for the folder to be based on. Default is the design of the default view of the database currently open. Blank is a blank design, and the remaining views and folders are those already in the current database.

4 To copy a folder from another database, open the database that contains the folder you want to copy. In the navigation pane, expand Design (select the triangle) and then select Folders.

5 Select the folder you want to copy in the view pane. Choose Edit, Copy to copy the view.

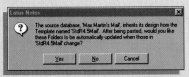

7 The folder now appears in the navigation pane under Views and Folders. If the folder you copied is part of a design template, you will receive a message that asks you if you want to keep the design of the folder in sync with the database folder you copied it from. To change the design of the folder select No; to keep the design the same select Yes. You can also cancel pasting the folder by selecting Cancel.

6 Now open the database you want to copy the view to. In the database's navigation pane, expand Design and then select Folders. Select the view pane and choose Edit, Paste. If the Paste option is grayed out, you did not successfully copy the view from the other database.

How to Manage Folders

Now that you know how to create a folder, here are some tips on how to manage folders. This section shows you how to put documents into a folder, remove documents from a folder, change the name of a folder, collapse and expand folders, move folders to different levels in the navigation pane, and delete folders.

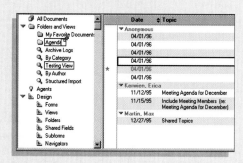

 1 To add documents to a folder, select and drag a document from the view pane over the folder name in the navigation pane and then let go of the mouse button. You can select more than one document when you want to move several documents to a folder.

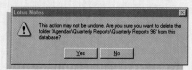

7 To delete a folder, select the folder in the navigation pane. Choose Actions, Folder Options, Delete Folder. Select Yes when you see the warning dialog box.

TIP SHEET

▶ When you delete a folder, keep in mind that the documents that were in the folder are not deleted from the database. Though the folder no longer appears in the navigation pane, the documents may appear in other views and/or folders. Documents in a database always appear in the All Documents view.

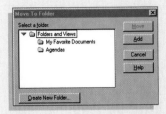

2 To use the menu to move a document into a folder, first select the document(s) in the view pane. Now choose Actions, Move To Folder. Select a folder to move the document(s) to, or create a new folder as the destination by selecting the Create New Folder button and following the same steps you normally would to create a new folder. Select Add to place the document(s) in the folder.

3 To remove documents from a folder, select the navigation pane and then the folder you want to remove one or more documents from (expand the folder if necessary to see a child folder). Select the documents that you want to remove from the folder. Go to the next step.

4 Choose Actions, Remove from Folder. Keep in mind that removing a document from a folder does not delete the document from the database. Edit, Clear would delete the documents from the database.

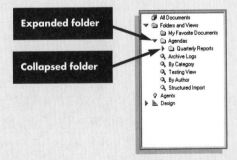

6 To change the name of a folder, select the folder in the navigation pane. Choose Actions, Folder Options, Rename. Enter the new name of the folder and click on the OK button. The name can be up to 64 characters in length.

5 To expand a folder, select the triangle to the left of the folder name while it is pointed to the right. To collapse a folder, select the triangle to the left of the folder name while it is pointed down.

CHAPTER 8

Reading, Creating, and Editing Documents

 Notes databases store information in documents. Each document can contain text, graphics, interactive objects such as buttons and hotspots, and sections for breaking down documents into logical segments.

You can read, edit, and create documents in a database provided you have sufficient access to the database (indicated in the ACL of the database). To review the access levels of a database, see the section "How to Find Information in a Database" in Chapter 5.

When you create and edit documents they are in *edit mode*. Edit mode enables you to enter information into fields in the document. The type of information that can be entered into a field depends on the type of field. There are text fields that take plain text, rich text fields that take formatted text and objects, number fields, and time fields. There are also keyword fields that are used to enter information based on data provided, as well as author, reader, and names fields that are used to identify users' roles within the document.

This chapter shows you how to read, open, edit, create, and save documents. These skills apply when using any Notes database, as well as your mail file (which is also a Notes database). Managing your mail documents is covered in detail in Chapters 10 and 11.

How to Read, Open, and Close Documents

Y ou can read a document from the three-paned database view, or you can open the document in its own window. This page shows you how to read a document, move around in a document, and adjust the display of a document.

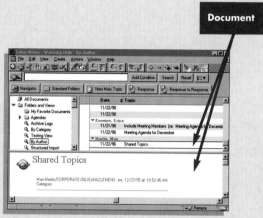

Document

1 There are two ways to read a document. The first way is to select the document in the view pane and then read it in the preview pane. If the preview is not open, choose View, Document Preview to open it.

11 You can close a document by pressing the Esc key (the esc key or Command+W on the Macintosh).

10 There are three kinds of links: document, database, and view links. Each links to a document, database, or view.

9 You can display an object's information by starting the object's application. Double-click on the object to open it. A section can be expanded and collapsed by clicking on it.

8 A file attachment can be opened (viewed) from within Notes, launched in the application it was created in, or saved (detached) to your local hard drive (or other disk). Double-click on the file attachment to open the Properties dialog box for it, and then click on the View, Launch, or Detach button to carry out one of these actions.

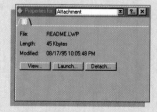

2 The second way to read a document is by opening it in its own window. You can do this by double-clicking on the document title in the view pane.

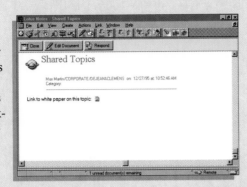

3 You can close the open document and read the next document without going back to the view pane. Make sure the open document is in read mode and then press the Enter key (return key on the Macintosh).

4 This is a document link. It leads you to another document that might be in the same database or another database. Select the link to view the document it links to.

Preview of document link

5 You can preview a document link in the preview pane. Select the link in the document and choose View, Document Link Preview.

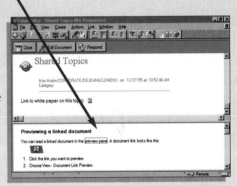

File attachment

OLE object

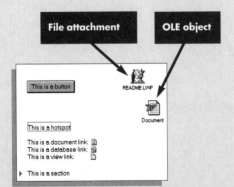

6 When you open a response document from the view pane, you can read its parent document in the preview pane. To do this choose View, Parent Preview.

Response document

Parent document preview

7 You can use objects you see in a document while the document is in read mode. A button performs a Notes action when pressed. A hotspot is an area of outlined text, and can display pop-up text or perform an action. A file attachment can be viewed, launched, or detached to a drive. An OLE object can be opened with its native application.

How to Create, Edit, and Save Documents

Now that you know how to read existing documents, here's how to create new documents. Once you create a document, it is open in edit mode. You can then add data, edit data, move around the document, and save the document.

1 To create a document in a database, first open the database. You can create a document by choosing from one of the forms available in the database. To view the available forms, open the Create menu. In this example, the forms include Main Topic, Response Or Comment, Response To Response, To Do, and Team Member.

▶ **A document is often designed to display the date and time that it was created and/or last modified. The date and time are taken from the server the database resides on, or in the case of a local database, the date and time are taken from the local workstation's date and time.**

▶ **To return to read mode when a document is open in edit mode, press Ctrl+E (or Command+E on the Macintosh).**

▶ **Fields that have red brackets are encrypted and require you to have the encryption key in order to read the contents of the field. Speak to the database manager or your Notes administrator about obtaining an encryption key.**

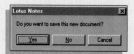

7 To save a document and close it, press the Esc key. You will be asked if you want to save your changes. Click on Yes to close the document and save your changes, No to close the document without saving changes, or Cancel to keep the document open without saving changes.

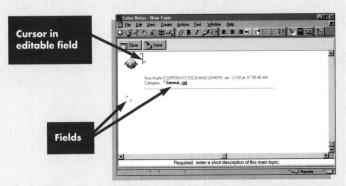

Cursor in editable field

Fields

② When you want to create a response document, you must first select the document you are responding to in the view pane. Then you can select the response form from the Create menu. In some databases, you can click on a button on the Action bar (the top of the window) to create a Response document automatically.

③ Once the new document is open you can add data to the fields. A field can be edited when there are brackets around it and the cursor can be placed in the field.

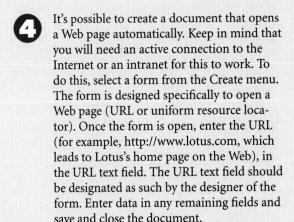

④ It's possible to create a document that opens a Web page automatically. Keep in mind that you will need an active connection to the Internet or an intranet for this to work. To do this, select a form from the Create menu. The form is designed specifically to open a Web page (URL or uniform resource locator). Once the form is open, enter the URL (for example, http://www.lotus.com, which leads to Lotus's home page on the Web), in the URL text field. The URL text field should be designated as such by the designer of the form. Enter data in any remaining fields and save and close the document.

⑥ While working in a document you can save it, protecting any work in progress. To do this, select File, Save, or press Ctrl+S (or Command+S on the Macintosh).

⑤ You can edit an existing document in one of several ways. One way is to select the document in the view pane and then choose Actions, Edit Document. Another way is to select the document and press Ctrl+E (or Command+E on the Macintosh). If the document is already open in read mode, you can double-click on the document to place it in edit mode. When the document is in the preview pane you can double-click on it to edit in the preview pane.

How to Copy, Paste, and Delete Data from a Document

You can copy, paste, and delete data from a document. Most often you are carrying out these actions in document fields while a document is open in edit mode. However, you can copy data from a document in both read and edit mode as long as the form was designed to allow you to do so.

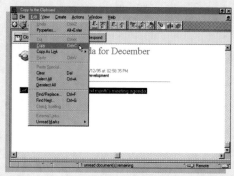

▶ ❶ You can copy data from one document to another or from one field to another. First, open the document you want to copy data from. Then, select the data and choose Edit, Copy. You can select data from a document in read mode or edit mode; however, sometimes different data is displayed depending on the mode the document is open in.

❼ When you press Enter (return on the Macintosh) or click on the button next to the keywords field, the Select Keywords dialog box appears, asking you to select from the available keywords. You can cycle through the keywords by pressing the spacebar. You can copy, cut, and paste keywords to and from a keywords field just as you do with other fields, provided you are not pasting rich text. In addition, the database designer may allow you to add new keywords in the "New Keywords" text box at the bottom of the dialog box.

2 To move data around in the same document or between two documents, select the data as in step 1 and choose Edit, Cut. A document must be in edit mode to cut data from it.

3 Now that you have copied (or cut) the data, you are ready to paste it into the document. Place the cursor in the field you want to copy the data into and choose Edit, Paste.

4 To delete data, select the data you want to delete and choose Edit, Clear. The document must be open in edit mode to delete data. Since deleting data is not reversible, consider cutting the data, which will store the cut data on the Clipboard until you copy or cut more data (overwriting the original data on the Clipboard).

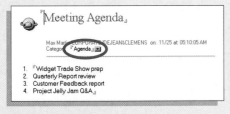

6 A keywords field might look like this field.

5 There are several kinds of fields found in a document. Two commonly used fields are plain text and rich text fields. You can copy data from both kinds of fields; however, you can only paste rich text data into rich text fields. Rich text includes formatted and styled text, graphics, tables, and objects (such as buttons and hotspots).

CHAPTER 9

Formatting Document Data

 As introduced in the previous chapter, Notes documents contain fields, and each field is a specific type. When creating documents in Notes, you can format the data you enter into rich text fields.

A Notes document rich text field can be treated just like text in a word processing document. Data in a rich text field may be formatted by adding and changing properties on a paragraph-by-paragraph basis.

Some of the things you can do to format rich text include changing the text's font, size, style, and color. In addition, you can align, indent, number, and add bullets to paragraphs. You can also insert page breaks, keep paragraphs on one page, set page margins with a ruler, set line spacing, hide paragraphs, and create style names to be reused. Notes also has a feature called *Permanent Pen* that you can use when adding comments to existing text.

Rich text fields can also hold graphics, tables, and interactive objects. Interactive objects include buttons, hotspots, sections, links, and file attachments, to name a few. Notes also allows you to spell check a document before you save and/or send it to a person or group of recipients. All these formatting techniques are covered in detail in this chapter. Once you have finished this chapter, practice your skills in the following Try It! exercise.

How to Format Rich Text

As you now know, there are both plain text fields and rich text fields in Notes, and both are used to enter and store data. A plain text field supports letters, whole numbers, punctuation, and spaces. A rich text field is just that: a rich environment supporting a full array of formatting features and objects. Here is how you format rich text data in Notes.

Font, size, and style name

Cursor in a rich text field

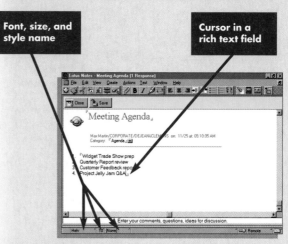

 1 To begin formatting rich text, open a document in edit mode and place the cursor in a rich text field. If you are not sure how to identify a rich text field, look at the Notes status bar. When the cursor is in a rich text field, the status bar displays the font, size, and named style of the current paragraph.

TIP SHEET

▶ **To shrink the Properties box so it shows just the top gray bar, double-click on the top gray portion of the infobox. You can also drag the top gray portion of the infobox to reposition the Properties infobox where you want it.**

▶ **The Hide tab has settings to hide paragraphs based on specific circumstances. You can also use the Notes formula language to enter a formula that hides a paragraph. The Notes formula language is used to design Notes databases, and is not covered in this book. Refer to the documentation and other books which cover designing and/or developing Notes databases and applications.**

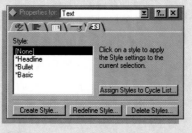

7 The Style tab has settings to assign named styles. To create a new style, select the paragraph you want to base the style on and then click on the Create Style button. To adjust a style's settings, select the paragraph you want to base the style on and then click on the Redefine Style button.

 You can use these menus on the status bar to change the font and size of rich text, as well as to apply named styles. Notes uses the fonts installed on your workstation. Any font style or size available in your font library or Fonts folder will be available in Notes.

To format new text, place the cursor where you are going to enter text. To format existing text, select the text. To choose from the full array of formatting options, select Text, Text Properties to open the Text Properties infobox.

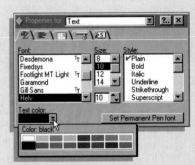

Each tab in the Properties infobox represents a group of formatting options. The Font tab has font, size, style, and color settings. This is also where you can set the style of the Permanent Pen font. To set the Permanent Pen font, select the font, size, style, and/or color you want it to be and then click on the Set Permanent Pen Font button. By default, the Permanent Pen is red bold. To use the Permanent Pen, place the cursor in a rich text field and choose Text, Permanent Pen.

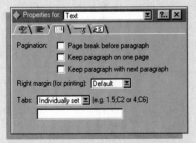

The Page tab allows you to adjust pagination, the right margin for printing, and tab stops.

The Alignment tab has settings to align text on a paragraph-by-paragraph basis.

How to Add Buttons, Links, Hotspots, and File Attachments

Now that you know how to format rich text, you can begin to add objects to your rich text fields. Objects can assist you in communicating and directing others to information contained in Notes databases. Adding these objects demonstrates why Notes documents are referred to as compound documents: They contain a combination of text and objects to store a rich set of information.

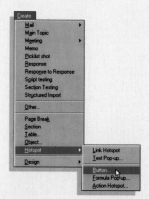

▶ **1** To create a button in a rich text field, place the cursor where you want the button to appear and choose Create, Hotspot, Button.

9 The same steps apply to creating a view or database link. Open the view, or open or select the database, and then choose Edit, Copy As Link, View Link, or Edit, Copy As Link, Database Link. The view link will open to the view. The database link will open to the database's default view or the last view you were in.

8 To create a document, database, or view link in a rich text field, you must first copy the link to the clipboard. To create a document link, go to the document and choose Edit, Copy As Link, Document Link.

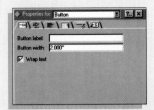

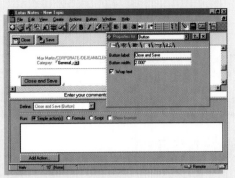

2 Add a label to the button in the Button Label text box. When you enter or edit the button title, a green checkmark to the right of the text box appears. Click on the green checkmark to confirm the title you have entered. You can also assign the width of the button and select Wrap Text to have the label text wrap to the next line of the button. The width of the button will be the length of the text or the Button width setting, whichever is shorter.

3 In the design pane you can determine what the button will do based on a simple action, formula, or script. You must know how to use the formula language or LotusScript to enter a formula or script; however, you can assign a simple action to the button without knowing these languages. Next to the Run options, choose Simple Action(s) and then click on the Add Action button located at the bottom left of the window.

4 In the Add Action dialog box, select an action to perform from the Action list.

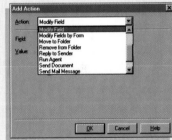

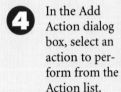

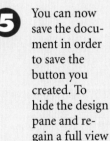

5 You can now save the document in order to save the button you created. To hide the design pane and re-gain a full view of the document, select the document. To go back to the design pane, choose Button, Edit Button while the button is selected. To close the Properties dialog box, select the diamond on the top left of the box and then select Close from the menu.

6 To create a hotspot, you must first select the text that the hotspot will encompass. Once the text is selected, choose Create, Hotspot. You have a choice of hotspots to create: a link hotspot, a text pop-up, a formula pop-up, or an action hotspot. In the case of a link hotspot, you will first have to copy a link to the Clipboard before you can create the hotspot. See how to create links later on this page. In this example, a text pop-up is created.

7 In the Properties infobox for the hotspot, type in the pop-up text that will be displayed. Although you create the pop-up text in the edit mode, you must be in the read mode to display the pop-up text.

How to Add File Attachments, Lists, and Sections and Set Paragraph Margins

File attachments are handy to store and distribute in Notes documents. Once in a document, a file attachment can be viewed, opened in its native application, or detached and saved to a disk. Lists and sections are useful ways of organizing information within a document, and simple to do. Setting paragraph margins allows you to adjust the margins in a single paragraph.

① To add a file attachment to a rich text field, place the cursor where you want the file attachment to go and choose File, Attach.

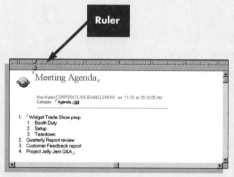

② You can also adjust a paragraph's margins with the ruler. Select the paragraph(s) and choose View, Ruler. On the ruler, drag the lower pointer to the position where you want the left margin to be for the selected paragraph(s). Drag the top pointer to indent the paragraph(s).

⑧ You can set paragraph margins in two ways: in the Text Properties infobox, or with the ruler. To use the Text Properties infobox, select the paragraph(s) you want to adjust and choose Text, Text Properties. Then select the Alignment tab. You can also set the margins for printing by selecting the Page tab. To set print margins for an entire page, choose File, Page Setup (on the Macintosh, choose File, Print and click on the Margins button).

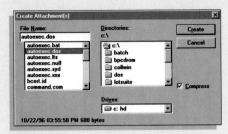

2 Choose a file to attach from the Create Attachment(s) dialog box. You can add two or more at the same time by holding down the Ctrl key while you select files (on the Macintosh, select each file one at a time, and click on the Open button). Click on the Create button to close the dialog box (the Done button on the Macintosh).

3 To create a bulleted list, place the cursor in the paragraph you want bulleted (to do two or more paragraphs, select all the relevant paragraphs) and choose Text, Bullets.

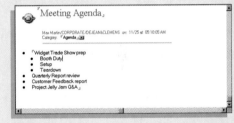

4 To indent a bulleted list within a bulleted list, select the paragraph(s) you want to indent and press F8, or choose Text, Indent.

5 To create a numbered list, select the paragraph(s) and choose Text, Numbers. To indent a numbered list within a numbered list, select the paragraph(s) you want to indent and press F8, or choose Text, Indent.

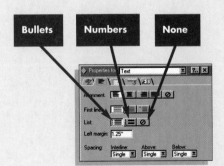

7 You can open the Properties infobox for a section to further customize it (such as giving it a title) by first selecting the section and then choosing Section, Section Properties.

6 You can also use the Text Properties box to apply a bulleted or numbered list style to a paragraph. Choose Text, Text Properties and then the Alignment tab. In the List options there is a bulleted button, a numbered button, and a button for no list creation.

How to Add Graphics and Tables and Spell Check a Document

Y ou can copy and paste or import graphics into a rich text field. You can also organize data in a table format. Spell checking your data is also important, and can be done in a document at any time while in edit mode.

 1 To paste a graphic into a rich text field, you must first copy it to the Clipboard. You can copy graphics from within Notes or outside of Notes. To copy a graphic from within Notes, select the graphic and choose Edit, Copy.

7 To spell check a document, open the document in edit mode and choose Edit, Check Spelling. To check just a selected portion of text, select the text and choose Edit, Check Spelling.

2 Once the graphic is copied to the Clipboard, place the cursor where you want the graphic to go and choose Edit, Paste.

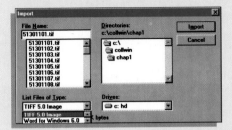

3 To import a graphic into a rich text field, place the cursor where you want the graphic to go and choose File, Import. Select the graphic you want to import from the Import dialog box (searching directories or folders if necessary). Select a graphic file type from the list of file types and then click on the Import button.

4 You can resize a graphic (when in edit mode) by selecting the graphic and then dragging the bottom right corner further out or in from where the graphic's original boundaries were.

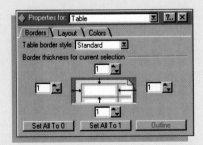

6 To adjust the formatting of a table, select the table (or place the cursor in a cell of the table) and choose Table, Table Properties. Use the Borders, Layout, and Colors tabs to adjust the table's layout.

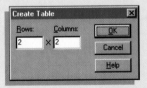

5 To create a table, place the cursor where you want the table to go and choose Create, Table. Set the number of rows and columns you want the table to have in the Create Table dialog box. Click on OK to create the table.

Now that you have learned how to create and format your own documents, let's put your skills to the test.

You will create a document, and in this document you will create a table to organize and hold file attachments. You will then save the document. Finally, you will create another document that holds a document link to the first document.

Open your mail database (or, if you do not use Notes mail, open a database you can create a document in).

Max Martin's Mail on Local

Create a new Memo document and place the cursor in the field (rich text field) below the Subject field.

Type in a sentence of text and then create a new paragraph (press Enter, or Return on the Macintosh).

Create a table
by choosing
Create, Table. Make a table with four
rows and two columns. Click OK.

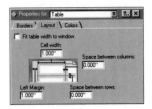

Go to the
Layout tab in
the Properties
infobox.
Deselect the Fit Table Width To
Window option and then make
the cell width 1 inch.

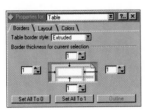

Open the Table
Properties
infobox.

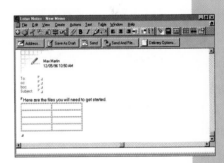

The first col-
umn of the
table will
contain the
name of
the file
attachment.

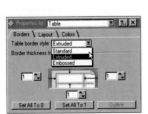

Change the
table border
style to
Extruded.

The file at-
tachment will
be attached
in the second
column of
the row. Type
in the name
of the first
file you will add to the table.

Continue to next page ▶

TRY IT!

Continue below

10

Tab over to the next column in the first row. The cursor should now be in the second column. Attach the file in the second column.

11

While the cursor is still in the second column, add a column by choosing Table, Append Column.

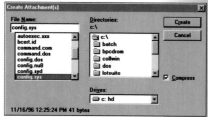

12

Add a description of the file attachment. Add another row containing another file name, the file attachment, and a description.

13

Enter a recipient name in the To field and enter a subject in the Subject field.

14

Save the file and close it. Select Save Only from the Close Window dialog box.

15

The document should now appear in the Drafts view and the All Documents view in your mail file.

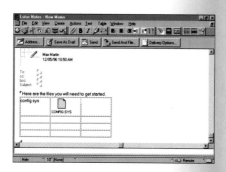

Open the document again.

Now create a new Memo document, placing the cursor in the field below the Subject field.

Switch to the first document you created and create a document link to this document.

Now switch back to the second document and paste the

document link into the rich text field below the Subject field. Fill out the To field and the Subject field as well, then save the document.

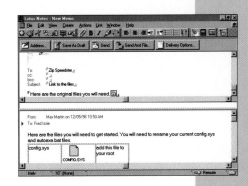

Now test the document link to make sure it leads back to the first document with the file attachments.

You can do this either by selecting the link or by viewing the link in the Document Link Preview pane.

CHAPTER 10

Using Notes Mail

 Notes mail, like other electronic mail (e-mail), allows you to communicate with other e-mail users. In Notes mail you can exchange mail, as well as other items that Notes supports such as file attachments, graphics, and other objects you place in rich text fields. To use Notes mail you must be connected to a network, either directly or remotely.

As you saw in the last Try It!, Notes mail is just like other Notes documents, so you will feel at home when you create, edit, and save Notes mail. This chapter will show you how to read, create, address, reply to, forward, and delete mail.

A Map of Your Mail File

When you open your mail database, you are presented with the three-pane view as in other databases; however, the navigation pane has some additional folders and views, which are pointed out here. For details on managing views and folders in your mail database, refer to Chapters 6 and 7.

 1 The Inbox folder contains all the mail you receive. A mail document stays in the inbox until you delete it or move it into another folder.

 Agents

11 These are the Agents in your database. Agents are covered in Chapter 16.

 Archiving

10 The Archiving view displays lists of documents you have archived. The process of archiving documents is detailed in Chapter 11.

 Discussion Threads

 9 The Discussion Threads view displays mail documents grouped together with their replies. This allows you to view whole conversations in order.

TIP SHEET

▶ **You can add folders (and views) to your mail database just as you would to any other Notes database. Keep in mind that you are the Manager (in the ACL) of your mail database.**

Drafts

2 The Drafts view displays all the mail you compose and save but have not yet sent. You can open mail in this view at any time, then edit it and/or send it. After you send mail from this view Notes places the document in the Sent folder. Stationery is also stored in this folder. You can discard a draft by marking the document for deletion.

 **Sent**

3 The Sent view displays mail you have both sent and saved. You can turn on the feature that allows you to send and save mail automatically in the User Preferences dialog box.

 All Documents

4 The All Documents view displays all the mail in your mail database.

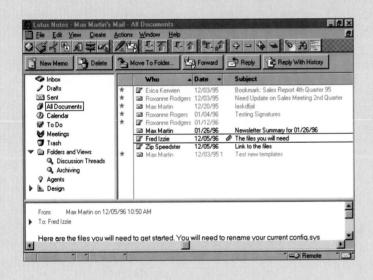

 Calendar

5 The Calendar view displays your calendar. This is covered in Chapter 11.

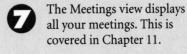 **To Do**

6 The To Do view displays all your tasks, categorized by their status, as well as any mail document that requires a reply before a certain date.

 Trash

8 The Trash folder displays mail you want to delete. Once you have dragged mail documents into this folder, you can then choose to delete them, or remove them from the Trash folder if you change your mind.

 Meetings

7 The Meetings view displays all your meetings. This is covered in Chapter 11.

How to Create, Save, and Send Mail

Here's how to manage your mail, whether you work on a network or remotely. Keep in mind that when you work remotely, your mail is saved in an outgoing mail database until it is ready to replicate with your mail server. If a preset number of messages are ready to be sent, Notes will initiate a call to the server and transfer the mail automatically. This is covered in greater detail in Chapter 12.

▶ **1** Open your mail database. If you are set up to work remotely, open your local mail database.

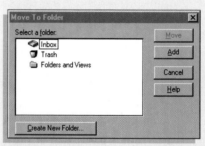

10 Alternatively, you can click on one of the Save buttons on the Action bar (Save As Draft, Send, or Send And File). The Save As Draft button automatically saves the memo to the Draft folder. The Send button opens the Close Window dialog box. The Send And File button first opens the Move To Folder dialog box where you can select or create a folder to add the memo to. Then it opens the Close Window dialog box so you can complete the mail send instructions.

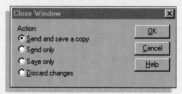

9 Press Esc to bring up the Close Window dialog box. You can now send the memo and save it, send it and not save it, save it and not send it, or leave it the way it was before you last saved it. If you have never saved your memo and choose Discard Changes, the memo will be deleted and not saved in the mail database.

2 Create a new mail memo by choosing Create, Memo. In the To field, enter the name of the person (or names of people and/or groups) you want to send the memo to.

3 There are several ways you can address a memo. One way is to just enter the name(s) and/or full address(es) of the recipient(s) if you know the correct spelling(s).

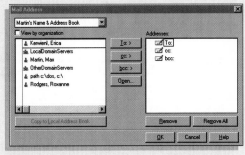

4 You can also click on the Address button (at the top of the Action bar) to enter addresses using the Mail Address dialog box. In the dialog box, you can use both Personal and Public Name and Address Books to select addresses to enter into the To, CC, and BCC fields.

5 Notes has a feature that makes addressing a memo as simple as entering just the first few letters of a recipient's name. To use this type-ahead addressing feature, in the To, CC, or BCC field, type the first few letters of a person's (or group's) name and Notes will enter a complete name. If this is not the name you want, keep typing; Notes will eventually find the name. Once Notes has found the name you want, press the Enter key to accept it. This feature works when you are connected to a network in order to access the server-based Name and Address Books, or if the person's name is in one of the address books that you have stored locally.

6 You can enter additional names in the CC and BCC fields. Note that BCC recipients' names are not seen by other recipients.

7 Enter a subject in the Subject field. Now click on the Delivery Options button (on the Action bar) to set your delivery settings for the memo. Delivery options are covered in detail on the next page.

8 Add a message to the field below the Subject field. Note that this is a rich text field, so you can take full advantage of Notes compound document features.

How to Customize Your Letterhead and Set Delivery Options

Notes lets you change the letterhead you use in your Memo and Reply forms. You can also set delivery options for receiving delivery reports, signing your mail, encrypting mail for security reasons, and a whole lot more. Here's how to set an array of mail options.

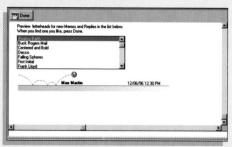

▶ **1** You may have a preference for a letterhead other than the default letterhead supplied by Notes. To change your letterhead, open your mail database (if it's not already open), and choose Actions, Mail Tools, Choose Letterhead. You can now preview the available letterheads for your Memo form and Reply form. When you're done, click on the Done button on the Action bar.

10 You can prevent recipients from copying data from the mail you send by selecting the Prevent Copying option. This feature not only prevents a recipient from copying data to the clipboard, but also guards against forwarding and printing the mail. It also keeps a recipient from including a history with a reply.

9 The Return Receipt option, when selected, will send you a message when a recipient reads mail you have sent.

▶ **You can have Notes automatically sign and encrypt your mail every time by selecting these settings in your User Preferences. For more details on how to set these options, see Chapter 2.**

▶ **To discard a mail message without saving it or sending it while creating or editing the mail message, press Esc or choose File, Close. In the Close Window dialog box that appears, select "Discard changes."**

▶ **You can see delivery information about a message sent to you by opening the message and choosing Actions, Deliver Information.**

8 You can select one of three options from the Delivery Priority pop-up menu. High sends you mail immediately. Normal sends your mail the next time the Notes server is scheduled to send mail. Low sends your mail on off-peak hours (as defined for the server; the default is between 12:00 AM and 6:00 AM).

2 To set delivery options for the current memo, click on the Delivery Options button on the Status bar, or choose Actions, Delivery Options.

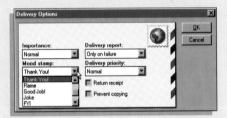

3 You can set the importance of your memo to Normal, High, or Low using the Importance pop-up menu. When the memo is set to High, an icon appears next to the memo in the recipient's mail database. When a memo is of high importance, it appears with a red envelope icon in the view pane.

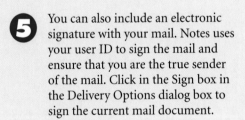

4 You can designate your memo as a particular type using the Mood Stamp option. Notes will display a different icon for each type of mood stamp except for the Normal type.

5 You can also include an electronic signature with your mail. Notes uses your user ID to sign the mail and ensure that you are the true sender of the mail. Click in the Sign box in the Delivery Options dialog box to sign the current mail document.

7 The Delivery Report option allows you to request a report from Notes, based on your selection. The Only On Failure option will send you a report when mail cannot be sent. The Confirm Delivery option will send you a report to let you know your mail was received. Trace Entire Path will send you a report of the path your mail took to reach the recipient(s). No reports will be sent when the None option is selected.

6 You can encrypt your mail by selecting the Encrypt option in the Delivery Options dialog box. This prevents your document from being read by someone other than its recipient(s). Check with your Notes administrator before encrypting mail. The differences between the North American and the International Versions (the encryption used) of Notes makes encrypted messages between them incompatible.

How to Set Special Mail Options and Enter Addresses in Your Address Book

There are additional options you can set for Notes mail. You can specify an expiration date to facilitate archiving and/or deleting documents, and you can stamp a memo to request that a recipient reply by a certain date. You can also retain the integrity of Notes mail when sending it through the Internet. These things are covered here, along with several things you can do to make addressing your mail quick and easy.

TIP SHEET

▶ To open the Mail Address dialog box at any time, choose Actions, Address.

▶ To tell Notes to use a different Personal Name and Address Book, choose File, Tools, User Preferences and click on the Mail icon. In the Local Address Books text box enter the name of each address book (the file name). Use a comma to separate each file name if you are entering more than one file name. Remember that the primary address book file name is NAMES.NSF. To find the path to an address book not in your Data directory (or folder), click on Browse.

▶ You can set your mail to be server-based or workstation-based, by selecting the option in your Location document. With server-based mail you use the mail file located on a server, directly. With workstation-based mail you use the mail file (local replica copy of your mail file) on your workstation. Choose File, Mobile, Locations, select the location and click on Edit Location (or choose Edit Current from the Location menu on your status bar). Go to the Mail section, and select either On server or Local. Click on the button to the right of the field to select one of these options.

▶ **1** There are two selections on the Actions menu you can utilize when creating and customizing your mail. The first set of options is accessible by choosing Actions, Special Options.

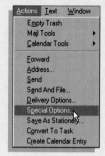

8 Enter the user's address in the Mail Address field. You can add optional information to the document as well. When you are finished, save and close the document.

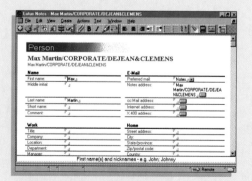

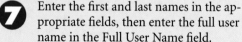

7 Enter the first and last names in the appropriate fields, then enter the full user name in the Full User Name field.

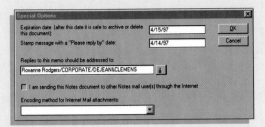

2 The first option in the Special Options dialog box allows you to set a date after which the document can be archived or deleted. This option stamps the mail with this expiration date.

3 You can also stamp the mail with a message that asks the recipient to reply by a certain date. In the Replies To This Memo Should Be Addressed To option, you can specify the name of a person or group, so that Notes sends the replies to someone else instead of to you.

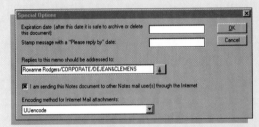

4 When you want to send mail through the Internet to another Notes user, you can preserve the formatting of the memo so that the recipient sees it as you do, instead of in plain text. Select the I Am Sending This Notes Document To Other Notes Mail User(s) Through The Internet option. If you are attaching files that you want to encode for a specific file format, select a file format from the Encoding Method For Internet Mail Attachments option.

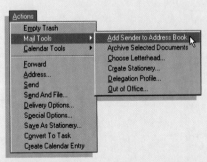

6 Another way to add addresses to your Personal Name and Address Book is by opening it and creating a Person document. To create a Person document, choose Create, Person.

5 Another area of options on the Action menu is accessible by choosing Actions, Mail Tools. The first option listed in the Mail Tools submenu, Add Sender To Address Book, allows you to add a sender's address to your Personal Name and Address Book automatically, by taking it from the current memo. To do this, open a memo (or select a memo in the view pane) sent by a person you want to add to your address book, then select this option. You can also select two or more memos in the view pane to add multiple senders' addresses all at once.

How to Reply to, Forward, and Delete Mail

Once you have received mail, you may want to reply to it, forward it to another person, delete it, or archive it. All four of these tasks are easily accomplished in your mail database. Here's how to do three of them. Archiving mail will be covered in the next chapter.

▸ **You can forward documents from databases other than your mail database by choosing Actions, Forward.**

▸ **You can tell Notes to notify you when you have new mail by selecting settings in the User Preferences. You can set an audible notification or a visible notification. See Chapter 2 for more details on how to set these preferences.**

▸ **You can edit an existing message just as you edit other Notes documents. Open the message in edit mode (select it in the view pane and press CTRL+E or Command+E on the Macintosh). Edit the message as you wish and then save and/or send the message. This is the way to edit messages in the Draft view.**

▸ **You can read messages that you have sent to other people and then forward or delete them. Open the Sent folder and then either forward it or delete it.**

▸ **1** To reply to a memo, have the memo open or selected in the view pane and choose Create, Reply or Create, Reply With History. The Reply form creates a regular reply memo, while the Reply with History form adds the original message at the bottom of the new reply memo.

8 To delete a memo while you have it open (and active), press the Delete key or click on the Delete button in the Action bar. Notes will mark the memo as deleted and then display the next memo.

7 Another way to mark a memo for deletion is to drag it from the view pane over to the Trash folder in the navigation pane. If you later decide you want to remove it from the Trash, open the Trash folder, select the memo, and choose Actions, Remove from Trash.

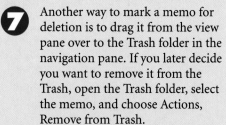

2 Compose and send the memo as you would with other memos.

3 To forward a memo to another person or group, first select or open the memo you want to forward, then choose Actions, Forward. Compose and send the memo as you would with other memos.

4 You can also forward two or more memos. To do this, select all the documents you want to forward (in a folder or view) and choose Actions, Forward. Notes creates a new memo that contains all the selected memos. Compose and send the new memo in the same way that you would send other memos.

5 To delete a memo from a view (and your mail database), you must first mark the memo for deletion. Then you can delete it from the database. Remember that removing a document from a folder does not delete it from the database.

6 To mark a document for deletion, select it and press the Delete key, or click on the Delete button on the Task bar. To delete the message from the database, choose Actions, Empty Trash. These steps also work for deleting multiple documents.

CHAPTER 11

Customizing Mail

 Now that you have covered the basics of using Notes mail, here are some ways to customize your mail and take further advantage of Notes mail features.

Apart from the standard Memo and Reply forms, you have use of several other forms for sending mail in alternative formats. These include a phone message, a Serial Routed memo, and a memo with a link automatically added to it.

Eventually, you will want to archive your mail to remove old, infrequently read, and expired mail from your mail database into an archive database. You can archive mail manually, or Notes can take care of it automatically.

Finally, you can assign and track tasks you need to execute, all from within your mail database. You can view the status of tasks, and even convert a mail document to a task. You can also assign a task to yourself or someone else. All this in your mail database! Here's how to use these features.

How to Create a Mailing List, Stationery, and Archive Mail

N ow that you know how to use your Personal Name and Address Book, you may find it useful to create a mailing list, which is two or more names (or other groups) saved as a group. A group name is entered into your address book, and then you can use it to address mail. In addition, you can create stationery for reusing mail layouts that you send often.

You may reach a point where you want to re-move memos from your mail database to reduce its size, as well as store the memos outside of your mail database. You can archive your mail to another database by marking mail to be archived.

TIP SHEET

▶ **To use your stationery, open the Draft view in your mail database and select the stationery you want to use. Click Use Stationery and Notes will create a new copy of the stationery document. The original stationery remains un-touched in your Drafts folder.**

▶ **To enable automatic archiving at any time, open the Archiving view in your mail database and click Enable Scheduled Archiving.**

▶ **Open your archive database from your mail database, open the Archiving view in your mail database and click on Open Archive Db.**

▶ **To initiate archiving files to your archive data-base, open the Archiving view in your mail database and click onArchive Now.**

▶ **To open and/or edit your Archive Profile docu-ment, open the Archiving view in your mail database and click on Setup Archive, or select the Archive Profile document in the view pane and press CTRL+E (Command+E on the Macintosh).**

▶ **① ** To create a group address in your Personal Name and Address Book, open the address book and choose Create, Group.

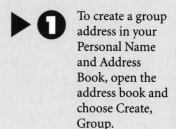

❾ To see your archived mail at any time, open the Archiving view. Once mail is archived to your archive database, it is no longer in the Archiving view. To view memos that have been saved to your archiving database, add your archive database to your workspace and open it.

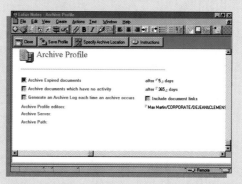

❽ Fill out the Archive Profile document to select criteria on which to base archiving of your mail. For help filling out the profile, select the Instructions button. Notes creates an archive database in your Notes Data directory (Data folder on the Macintosh). To specify the file name and where to save the archive database, select the Specify Archive Location button on the Action bar. When you have completed the profile, save it and close it. To make changes to the Archive Profile document, come back to this view and select the Setup Archive button again.

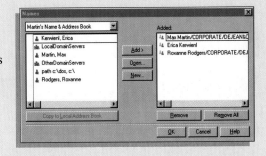

2 Enter the name of the group (whatever you want to call it) in the Group Name field by first clicking on the button to the right of the field. Then enter the type of group in the Group Type field. Multipurpose is the most useful, unless you want to restrict your use of the group name to Access Control List, Mail, or Deny List only.

3 Enter the names of the members in the Members field. Select the button next to this field to add names directly from address book(s). Save and close the document and your Personal Name and Address Book. You can now use the group name when addressing mail.

4 To create stationery, first create a memo with the format and recipients you want. Then choose Actions, Save As Stationery.

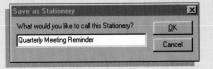

5 Enter the name of the stationery and select the OK button. The memo will now be saved as stationery in the Drafts folder. To create a memo from stationery, open the Drafts folder, select the stationery under the Stationery category, and choose Actions, Use Stationery.

6 You can also create your own stationery, with a customized header and footer, adding your own text and/or graphics such as a company logo or letterhead. To do this, choose Actions, Mail Tools, Create Stationery, and then select Personal Stationary and OK. Enter the header information in the field at the top of the document, and enter the footer information in the field in the bottom of the document. Save and close the newly created stationery. Use it the same way you use regular stationery, by choosing it from the Drafts folder.

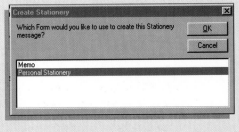

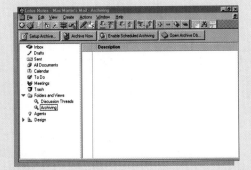

7 You can set up your mail so that Notes archives memos based on specific criteria. First, set up your archive profile by opening the Archive view and selecting the Setup Archive button on the Action bar.

How to Create Special Types of Mail

You have already seen how to create mail using the Memo, Reply, and other supporting memo forms under the Create menu. In this section you'll learn how to create other types of mail using some special forms. These forms will allow you to create a phone message, send a message with a link to another document, let people know when you will be out of the office, and send a message sequentially.

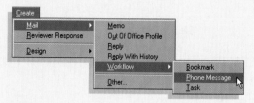

▶ ① You can create a message that tells someone that they have received a phone call. From your mail database, choose Create, Special, Phone Message. When you are in another database, choose Create, Mail, Workflow, Phone Message.

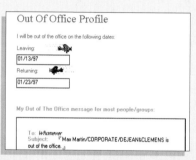

8 Enter the dates you are leaving and returning on, and make any changes you need to make to the subject of the message in the My Out Of The Office Message For Most People Or Groups field. When you are done, click on the Enable Out Of Office Agent button. Notes asks you to choose a server to run it on—select your mail server and then select OK. To stop running your Out Of Office memo, choose Actions, Mail Tools, Out of Office and click on the I Have Returned To The Office button.

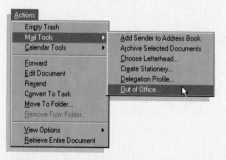

7 Another form allows you to respond to mail while you are out of the office. Notes sends a reply you have formulated, telling the sender(s) when you will return. To do this, you will need to have proper access to run agents on your mail server, so check with your Notes administrator to make sure this is set for you. To create an Out of Office memo, choose Actions, Mail Tools, Out of Office.

TIP SHEET

▶ **When using the Out of Office memo, Notes sends only one message to a single recipient regardless of how many messages they have sent you. On your return date, Notes sends you a welcome back message containing a list of all the senders' names. Don't forget to disable the memo when you get back to Notes.**

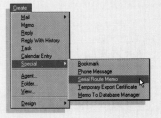

3 You can create a memo that is sent sequentially to a list of recipients. Each recipient can add comments to the memo and then send the message to the next person. To do this from your mail database, choose Create, Special, Serial Route Memo. To do this from another database, choose Create, Mail, Other, Serial Route Form.

4 Enter the names of the recipients in the Route To field. Note that this field does not accept group names. For help in adding names to this field, choose Actions, Address. Fill out the remaining information in the memo and optionally, select Notify Sender At Each Stop if you want to receive a message each time each recipient receives the message. To save and send the message, click on the Send To Next Person button on the Action bar.

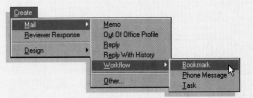

5 You can create a memo (called a Bookmark) that automatically links to a document in another database. This allows the recipient to view the linked document while reading your memo. Keep in mind that the recipient must have sufficient access to the database and the document being linked to. To create a memo with a link, open the database containing the document being linked to, then select the document and choose Create, Mail, Workflow, Bookmark.

---

2 Enter the appropriate information about the phone call. Enter the name of the person who called in the Contact field. You can also set delivery options for the phone message by clicking on the Delivery Options button. When you are done, save and send it like you send other mail.

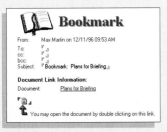

6 The Bookmark memo contains the link, the subject of the memo, and link information. Enter the recipient's name(s) in the To field (and CC and BCC fields if you want to), then save and send it like other mail.

How to Assign and Track Tasks

Y ou can create tasks for yourself and for others to complete. You can also track and manage these tasks, entirely in your mail database. Notes can update the status of a task until it is complete or deleted. You also have the option of displaying the task in your calendar. Here is how to create and track tasks in your mail database.

▶ **To delete a task, open the To Do view and select one or more tasks that you want to delete. Click Delete. Notes asks you if you want to delete the task if it has not been deleted. Notes adds the task to your Trash folder. Press F9 or close and open the database again to see that the task(s) has been deleted, however be aware that Notes will delete all documents in your Trash folder, not just the deleted task(s).**

▶ **If you your calendar displays a task and you want to remove it from your calendar, open the To Do view and double-click on the task entry you want to remove. Click Edit Task. In the task window, click Remove From Calendar View.**

 1 To assign a task to yourself while in your mail database, choose Create, Task. When in another database, choose Create, Mail, Workflow, Task.

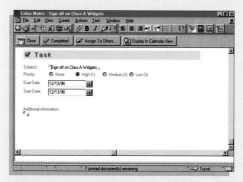

8 To edit a task, double-click on the task in the view pane. Now click on the Edit button in the Action bar. You can edit any of the fields in the task, mark the task as completed, assign it to others, and/or display it in your Calendar view.

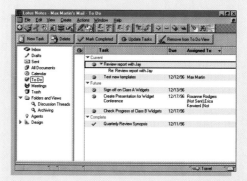

7 Select the To Do view from the navigation pane in your mail database. The memo now appears in the To Do view with other tasks. Notice that the Action bar has several buttons to carry out actions related to your tasks. Note that when you update and complete tasks, they are displayed in the correct categories in the To Do view (since the last time you edited the tasks).

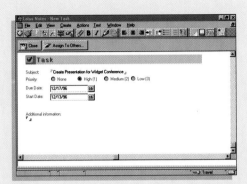

2 Enter the task title in the Task field. You can set a priority for the task, which will show up in the To Do view as either 1 (high), 2 (medium), or 3 (low).

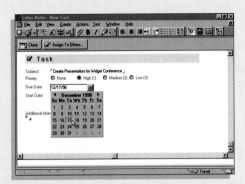

3 Enter the due date and the start date for the task. Click on the calendar icon to select the date directly from a calendar. When the start date is after today's date the task appears in the Future category in the To Do view in your mail database.

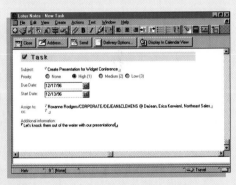

4 At this point, the task is assigned to you. You can save it or send it, or you can assign the task to others by clicking on the Assign To Others button on the Action bar. Now the task appears with the Assign To field displayed.

6 To convert a memo to a task, open a memo, or select it in the view pane, choose Actions, Convert To Task. You can now edit it to adjust any task information. Notes changes the subject of the memo into the Task field and the body of the memo into the Additional Information field.

5 Fill in the Assign To field. The CC field is optional. You can add a description or comments to the task in the Additional Information field. To save the task without sending it, click on the Close button; otherwise click on the Send button.

CHAPTER 12

Scheduling Meetings and Appointments

 Notes mail has two views, the Calendar view and the Meeting view, that are used to create and view your scheduled meetings, appointments, invitations, reminders, events, and anniversaries.

The Calendar view is an interactive calendar where you can view and schedule the current week's calendar entries, or skip a week, month, or a year ahead to view and schedule far in advance. The Meetings view displays your calendar entries in the familiar tabular list formation that other views display. From the list you can open an entry as an individual document, edit it, save it, and/or delete it.

This chapter shows you how to use the Calendar and Meetings views, create calendar entries, and manage your appointments. You can use the Calendar feature whether you are a network or remote user, so take advantage of this unique feature built into your mail database.

A Map of the Calendar View

The Calendar view displays a week at a time; however, you can easily display a week forward, a week back, or a month back or forward. You can also view the calendar and preview the currently selected calendar entry.

▶ **1** Open your mail database (if it is not already open) and select the Calendar view.

10 To view all appointments (entries) and responses to them, select the Meetings view.

9 When you have skipped forward or backward in dates, you can easily return to the current date by clicking on the Go To Today button on the Action bar.

8 To view a calendar entry in the preview pane, select the entry and choose View, Document Preview. You can preview an entry in the Two Day, One Week, Two Week, and One Month Calendar views.

TIP SHEET

▶ **The bottom of the calendar tells you how many weeks are left in the year. Notes tells you how many months are left in the year in the One Month view of the calendar.**

2 Each day has a clock icon. When you click on the clock icon, it displays the day's hourly slots, from 7:00 AM to 7:00 PM. Hold down the up or down arrow key to scroll through the hourly slots.

3 You can select the turned-up page at the bottom right or left of a day to flip forward or back through the days of your calendar.

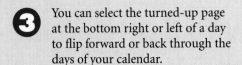

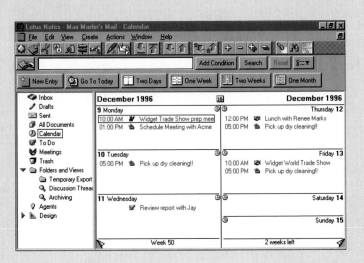

4 To move a month ahead, select the calendar icon on the top of the calendar. To move a forward a month (or more) click on the right arrow; to move back a month (or more) click on the left arrow. Click on a day in another week to jump to that day.

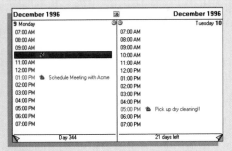

5 To focus in on a particular day's schedule, double-click on the date or click on the Two Days button on the Action bar.

7 To view a month at a time, click on the One Month button on the Action bar. The one month button on the Action bar may be at the very right edge or off the bar, depending on your screen resolution. Alternatively, you can select View, Calendar, One Month from the toolbar.

6 To view two weeks at a time, click on the Two Weeks button on the Action bar.

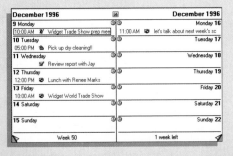

How to Set Up Your Calendar and Delegation Profile

The first thing you will do when you begin using your Calendar (and Meeting) view is set up a Calendar Profile. Your Calendar Profile can be edited at any time from your mail database.

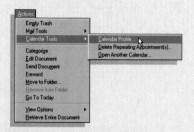

▶ **1** To access the Calendar Profile document from the menu, choose Actions, Calendar Tools, Calendar Profile.

8 Expand the Advanced Calendar Options (expand this section) to set automatic actions and entry options. You can automatically process meetings and remove meeting invitations after responding to them. You can set the default calendar entry type for each new entry you create, and you can select an option that hides new calendar entries from public view. You can also ask Notes to alert you (with the alarm) about scheduling conflicts with appointments in your calendar.

7 Scroll down to the Freetime Options section. The Freetime Options allow you to restrict who can read your free time schedule in your calendar (click on the button to the right of the first field to select people from an address book), and also allows you to schedule which hours and days your free time encompasses. This helps others to schedule meetings around your free time.

TIP SHEET

▶ When you select to automatically process meetings, Notes automatically schedules a meeting when the meeting fits into your free time. If you enter in names in the **Autoprocess Meetings Only From The Following People** field, Notes automatically schedules a meeting for you when you are invited by one or more of those people.

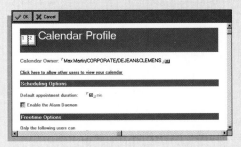

2 In the Calendar Profile document, the first field is the Calendar Owner. This is usually just you. However, if you want other people to be added to the profile and to be able to edit the profile, enter each person or group's name here, separating the names with commas. Click on the button to the right of the Calendar Owner field to add names via your address book(s).

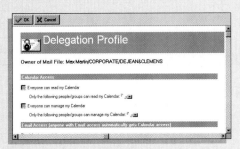

3 To allow other users to see and use your calendar, click on the line which reads Click here to allow other users to view your calendar. This will open your Delegation Profile.

4 You can allow everyone to read your calendar, or restrict access to certain people and/or groups. Likewise, you can allow everyone to manage your calendar (including the ability to create and edit entries), or only allow certain people and/or groups that kind of access.

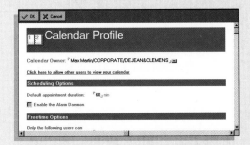

6 You are now back in your Calendar Profile. In the Scheduling Options section, select the options you desire. The appointment duration is the amount of time given for an appointment by default (60 minutes), but note that this value can be changed when you set up an appointment. The Alarm (Enable The Alarm Daemon) notifies you of an appointment when you have set the alarm for a particular calendar entry. See the next page for details on setting an alarm for a calendar entry.

5 Scroll down the Delegation Profile to the Email Access section. Note that any person to whom you give e-mail access automatically gets Calendar access. You can enter the names of people and/or groups who can read your mail, send mail on your behalf, edit documents in your mail file, and delete mail. When you have finished editing your Delegation Profile, press Esc (on the keyboard).

How to Use Your Calendar

N ow that you know your way around your calendar, here's how to use your calendar to set up meetings, appointments, and other scheduled events, thus helping you organize your time.

▶ **1** To create a calendar entry using the menu, choose Create, Calendar Entry. To create an entry from the Calendar view, select the day from the view pane (whether you are in the two day, one week, two week, or one month view of your calendar), and then click on the clock icon. Next, either double-click on a time to create the entry, or select the New Entry button on the Action bar.

TIP SHEET

▶ **You can copy and paste appointments between days. Select the appointment you want to copy and choose Edit, Copy. Now select the day you want to paste the appointment into and choose Edit, Paste.**

▶ **You can move Calendar entries by dragging and dropping them into other dates. Click and hold the entry and then drag it on to the turned-page icon on the bottom right or left of the Calendar page. Keep turning the pages until you find the date you want to move the entry to and then place the entry in that day.**

▶ **When editing a calendar entry, you can check the view of your calendar in a single window by clicking on the Check Calendar button on the Action bar.**

▶ **You can change the day, week, or month the Calendar View is currently displaying by choosing options from the View, Calendar menu. You can also go to a particular date by choosing View, Calendar, Go To. To go to the current date, choose View, Calendar, Go To Today.**

9 You can access another person's calendar by choosing Actions, Calendar Tools, Open Another Calendar. In the Open Calendar dialog box, select a person and click on the OK button.

8 When you are ready to save the entry, click on the Save and Close button on the Action bar, or press Esc.

7 To edit the frequency of, or delete a repeating appointment, select the appointment and choose Actions, Calendar Tools, Delete Repeating Appointment(s). In the Change Repeating dialog box, you can delete just the selected appointment, all of the remaining appointments, all previous appointments, or all future appointments.

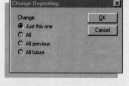

2 Select the type of entry from the radio buttons at the top of the document: Appointment, Invitation, Event, Reminder, or Anniversary. Each entry type displays slightly different options. Each type is also displayed with a different icon next to it in the calendar view.

3 Enter a brief description of the appointment, which will appear in the Calendar view. To change the date, click on the calendar icon next to the Date field. To change the time, click on the clock icon next to the Time field.

4 The Invitation entry allows you to plan a meeting and invite Notes users. Enter the names of the people (or groups) invited, or click on the button next to the Send Invitations To field to use the address book(s). Note that you can add optional invitees and select whether you want responses from those invitees.

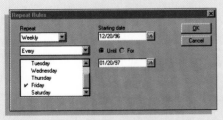

6 To schedule an appointment on a regular basis, you can create a repeating entry. Click on the Repeat button on the Action bar. Notes will automatically enter the appointment weekly, monthly by date, monthly by day (of the week), yearly, or as you specify in the Repeat Rules dialog box.

5 If you enabled the setting in your Calendar Profile document so that you are using the alarm settings, you can set or adjust your alarm settings for a particular entry by clicking on the Alarm Options button on the Action bar (top of the calendar entry). If you 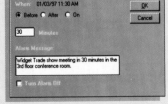 have not enabled it, Notes will ask you if you want to enable when you select Alarm Options. You can set the alarm before, after, or at a specific date and time by selecting "On," and you can enter the number of minutes for the alarm to go on before or after the appointment time. The alarm message is the entry's description (by default), unless you enter a different alarm message in the text box below "Alarm Message." You can cancel the alarm at any time by opening the calendar entry in edit mode, click on Alarm Options and select the "Turn Alarm Off" option.

CHAPTER 13

Using Mobile Notes

 Working as a mobile user allows you to work in Notes while disconnected from a Notes server. You call a Notes server when it's convenient (or necessary) and replicate updates to your mail database and other databases. You can read updated information at your own pace, in any place you can take your computer or laptop, without being online with the Notes server.

To use Notes remotely (that is, away from a network), you must be in remote setup and have a modem to call (dial) a Notes server. To review remote setup procedures, refer to Chapter 1.

This chapter will show you how to set up your modem, enter phone numbers, set up server connections, edit and create Location documents, call a server, create local replicas, and replicate your mail. The next chapter continues where this chapter leaves off, introducing you to the Replicator and showing you how to replicate databases.

How to Set Up Your Modem

Before you can work remotely in Notes, you need to set up your modem. Although this may have already been handled during your remote Notes setup (covered in Chapter 1), this page will help you verify that you have set up your modem correctly. In addition, if you need to change modem settings, you can see how and where to enter these changes.

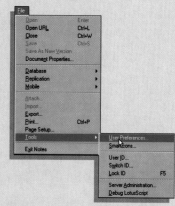

▶ **1** To set up your modem, choose File, Tools, User Preferences.

11 For Windows, OS/2, and UNIX users, the Port number is the number that identifies the current port. For example, COM1 is port 1.

10 The Dial Timeout option allows you to control how long (in seconds) Notes will attempt to connect with the server before giving up. The Hangup If Idle For option allows you to determine how long Notes waits before hanging up when it does not sense activity or communication between you and the server. This is measured in minutes.

9 The Hardware Flow Control option, when enabled, controls the flow between your modem and the Notes server's modem. To use this option you need a modem and/or cable that supports hardware flow control.

TIP SHEET

▸ **Your Notes administrator may advise you to use a script when you use your modem (the script is given to you as a file, which you place on your workstation). To select or edit a script (editing a script requires knowledge of the Hayes modem command language), click on Acquire Script in the Additional Setup dialog box. For more information on using scripts, ask your Notes administrator for assistance.**

▸ **The Log modem I/O and Log script I/O options are used when you are having modem problems. By selecting the Log modem I/O option, you record modem control strings and call responses in the Miscellaneous Events view of your Notes Log database (in your Data directory; file name is LOG.NSF). If you use a script to communicate, select the Log script I/O option so you will log problems in the log database just as you would with the Log modem I/O setting.**

2 Select Ports in the User Preferences dialog box. Now select the port your modem is connected to under Communication Ports (usually COM1 or COM2).

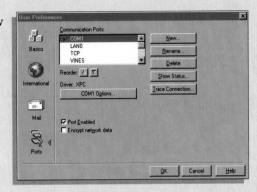

3 Enable the port by selecting the Port Enabled option.

4 Select the Port Options button, which will have the port name along with Options (such as COM1 Options).

5 In the Additional Setup dialog box, scroll down the Modem Type menu and select the modem type you have. If your modem is not listed, select one that is close to it, such as the same brand name and/or speed. Alternatively, you can select Auto Configure if your modem is a Hayes-compatible modem.

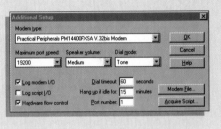

6 In the Maximum Port Speed menu, select the highest speed your modem supports. Keep in mind that the maximum speed you can connect to a server at is determined by the modem on the other end of the line and/or the operating system you are using.

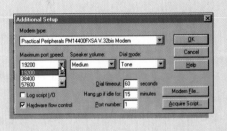

7 The Speaker Volume setting allows you to hear the call while it is in progress. You can set the modem speaker to Low, Medium, or High; or Off if you do not want to hear the modem.

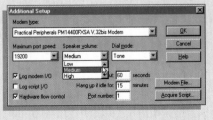

8 The Log Modem I/O option records modem responses in the Miscellaneous Events view of your local Notes log database. Use the log to troubleshoot when you are having difficulty making a connection with the modem. To open your Notes log, choose File, Database, Open and look for the database with the file name LOG.NSF.

How to Create a Server Connection

In order to call a Notes server, you need to set up a Server Connection document in your Personal Name and Address Book. These steps show you how.

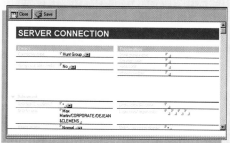

1 To create a new Server Connection document, open your address book and choose Create, Server Connection.

8 When your workgroup/organization has set up a hunt group(s) for a passthru server(s), you can use the hunt group to connect to two or more passthru servers with a single remote call. A hunt group is a group of servers associated with the same phone number (for dial-in purposes). To create a Connection document for a hunt group, in the Server Connection document enter **Hunt Group** in the Connection Type field. Enter the hunt group name in the Hunt Group Name field. Also enter the phone number and other information to complete the Server Connection document. You may need to obtain this information from your Notes administrator.

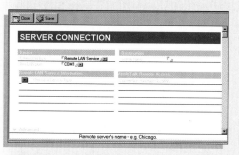

7 You can use a remote LAN service, such as AppleTalk Remote Access or Microsoft Remote Access Service, to connect to a server. To create this type of server connection, enter **Remote LAN Service** in the Remote LAN Service field. Also enter a port to use, your login name, your password, and the phone number of the remote LAN server. You may need to obtain this information from your Notes administrator and/or your network administrator.

2 To edit an existing Server Connection document, double-click on it in the view pane. You can also add or edit a Server Connection document by choosing File, Mobile, Server Phone Numbers. This will open the Server Connections view in your Personal Name and Address Book.

3 You are now ready to enter the connection type, server name, country code, area code, and phone number of the server. You may need to obtain some of this information from your Notes administrator.

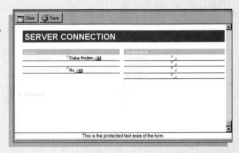

4 To set up a dial-up server connection (using your modem), enter **Dialup Modem** in the Connection Type field. You can select from the Connection Type field keywords by clicking on the button next to it (opening the Select Keywords dialog box).

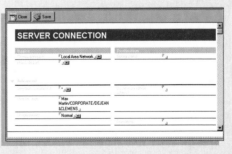

5 When you are in the office (connected to a local area network), you may want to connect to a server over the network. In this case, enter **Local Area Network** in the Connection Type field. Enter the port type as well in the Use LAN Port field. Make sure your network port is enabled (in the User Preferences). You can quickly edit the port for the current location by choosing File, Mobile, Edit Current Location.

6 You can access other Notes servers by "passing through" the server you have a connection to. To do this you need to create a Passthru Server Connection document. The servers you connect to via passthru are called destination servers. To create a passthru connection, in the Server Connection document, enter **Passthru Server** in the Connection Type field. Also specify the name of the passthru server in the Passthru Server Name field.

How to Call a Notes Server

There is more than one way to connect to a Notes server using a modem. You can dial the server's phone number automatically, or use an operator to assist you in obtaining an outside line to call a Notes server. Of course, in both of these cases you can hang up the call when you have completed what you set out to do during the remote connection.

▶ **You can insert one or more commas in the Phone Number field of the Server Connection document to delay dialing. Each comma represents a two-second delay. This is useful when you know there is a delay while dialing the number on the other side. Conversely, Notes ignores hyphens and dashes in a phone number.**

▶ **You can enter more than one phone number for a server. In the Phone Number field, enter each phone number, separating them with semicolons. When you try to connect, Notes will allow you to choose between all the numbers you have listed.**

▶ **You can use a different phone number than the one appearing in the Server Number text box by typing it in manually.**

▶ **1** To have Notes call a server automatically, choose File, Mobile, Call Server.

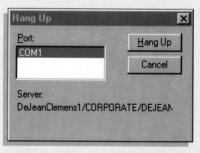

7 To hang up the call, choose File, Mobile, Hang Up, and then click on the Hang Up button.

2 Select the server you want to call from the Call Server dialog box and then click on the Auto Dial button. Notes will dial the server and tell you the progress of the call in the Status bar. If you have a remote LAN service connection setup, the remote connection option will also appear in the Call Server dialog box along with the list of servers.

3 If you need operator assistance when dialing a server number, choose File, Mobile, Call Server and then click on the More Options button in the Call Server dialog box.

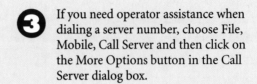

4 Click on the Manual Dial button. Pick up the phone and dial the operator when Notes tells you to. The phone must be connected to the phone port on your modem and the line from the wall for that phone must be plugged into your line port on the modem. Be cautious when plugging a phone line into your modem card, since digital phone lines can damage your modem. Always confirm that you are using an analog phone line, and not a digital (PBX), party, or coin telephone.

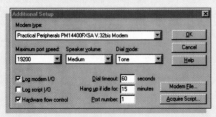

5 Once you are connected to an outside line, dial the server number. Dialing manually in this way is useful when you have to first enter a dialing prefix for a calling card, or need someone to obtain an outside line for you before you dial.

6 To adjust the port and/or modem settings for the call, click on the More Options button. To change the port, hold down the arrow next to the Port text box. To adjust modem settings, click on the Setup button. This dialog box will appear.

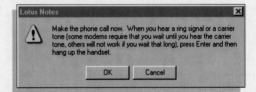

How to Create a Location

A *location* is a document in your Personal Name and Address Book used by Notes to figure out how to connect to a server, whether you are working remotely (mobile Notes user) or on a network. When you go through the setup procedure, Notes creates five Location documents for you in your address book: Island (disconnected), Home (modem), Office (network), Travel (modem), and Internet (modem and network). You can edit these Location documents or create new ones.

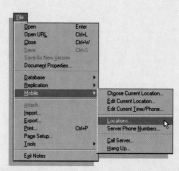

▶ **1** To edit one of your current Location documents, either choose File, Mobile, Locations, or open your Personal Name and Address Book and then the Locations view.

11 The Ports section displays the ports currently enabled. Select one or more ports to use at this location in the Ports section. You can enable other ports in your User Preferences (choose File, Tools, User Preference). If this is a mobile location, enter the phone dialing information. Enter the remaining information in the Mail and Replication sections of this location.

10 Under the Servers section, enter the name of your mail or home server, and/or a passthru server.

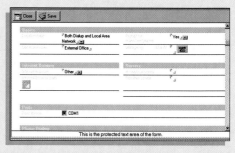

9 If you have chosen to use a browser other than Notes, your Location document will look like this. Click on the Internet Browser Path button (flashlight icon) to indicate where your browser resides on your local drive.

TIP SHEET

▶ **You can access the Web using either the Personal Web Navigator or the Server Web Navigator. The Personal Web Navigator is used when you have the proper protocols installed on your workstation, and a connection to the Internet. The Server Web Navigator is used when you access a Notes server in order to access the Internet. If you are unsure of which one to use, speak to your Notes administrator.**

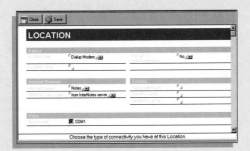

2 You can also edit your current Location document, or another Location document, by selecting it from the Status bar at the bottom of the screen.

3 In the Basics section, enter the location name, which can be any name you choose. Pick a name that helps you identify when you want to use this location.

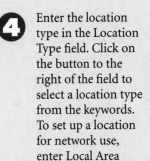

4 Enter the location type in the Location Type field. Click on the button to the right of the field to select a location type from the keywords. To set up a location for network use, enter Local Area Network. To set up a location for mobile use, enter Dialup Modem. To set up a location for both network and mobile use, enter Both Dialup and Local Area Network. To set up a location without a connection, enter No connection.

5 Enter the name of the location, such as Travel, Hotel, or Office, in the Location Name field. In the Prompt For Time/Date/Phone field, enter Yes if you want Notes to ask you information regarding this location's information. Otherwise, enter No so that you are not prompted.

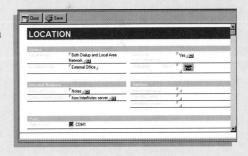

6 If you have chosen Local Area Network as your location type, the Web Proxy field appears in the Basics section. Use this field to connect to the Web through a proxy server. Click on the button to the right of the field (with the cap icon) and enter the appropriate information. You may need to obtain the proxy server information from your Notes or network administrator.

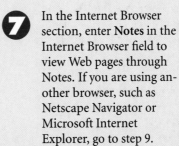

7 In the Internet Browser section, enter **Notes** in the Internet Browser field to view Web pages through Notes. If you are using another browser, such as Netscape Navigator or Microsoft Internet Explorer, go to step 9.

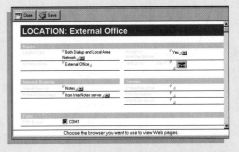

8 In the Retrieve/Open Pages field, click on the button next to the field to retrieve Web pages from an InterNotes server, from your workstation, or choose not to retrieve them. If you select to retrieve pages from an InterNotes server, enter the name of the server in the InterNotes Server field in the Server section.

How to Choose and Edit a Location

You may find that you work with Notes at more than one location, possibly even three or four locations. For example, you may work in the office, work while traveling, and work at home sometimes. In addition, you may need a location set up for times when you are in a hotel or a location you are at infrequently. You can switch between the Location documents you have set up so that it is quick and easy to change your location setting in Notes at any time.

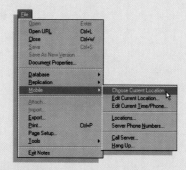

 One way to select a location is by choosing File, Mobile, Choose Current Location.

▶ You can update time and area code settings for the current location at any time (for example, if you use the same location document in different places). Choose File, Mobile, Edit Current Time, Phone.

▶ To see a list of all your server phone numbers with their associated locations, choose File, Mobile, Server Phone Numbers.

▶ You can specify a user ID file that Notes should use (or switch to) for a particular location. For example, you may be at a certain location infrequently and require a user ID authorized for the servers at this particular location. To do this, choose File, Mobile, Locations, select the location and click on Edit Location. Expand the Advanced section in the location document and enter the path and name of the user ID file in the User ID To Switch To field.

2 You can also select a location from the Status bar.

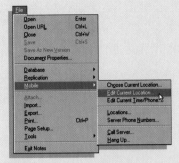

3 One way to edit the current location is by choosing File, Mobile, Edit Current Location.

4 Another way to edit the current location is by choosing Edit Current from the Status bar.

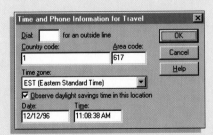

6 In the Time And Phone Information dialog box for your current location, enter or edit information in the appropriate fields. Then click on OK to close the dialog box and save the changes to the location.

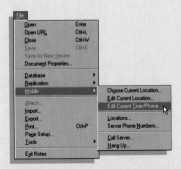

5 You can edit your current location's time and phone information by choosing File, Mobile, Edit Current Time/Phone.

CHAPTER 14

Using the Notes Replicator and Replicating Databases

 Notes allows you to replicate databases that are replica copies, so you can synchronize and update more than one copy of a single database. Replication also allows you to store the same information on many servers and workstations, including your own workstation!

The Notes replication process exchanges database modifications between two *replica* copies. A replica is an exact copy of a master database that exists on a Notes server. To keep these copies in sync, Notes runs a procedure called *Replication* in which it updates both the master and the replica with any changes that have been made to either since the last update. Certain databases can be accessed by many people, several of whom may have their own local replica copies of the database. Notes will keep track of all changes made to replicas and keep all of them in sync.

Each replica copy has an identical replica ID. Replication can occur between two servers, or between a server and a workstation. When replication occurs between a server and a workstation, the workstation must initiate the replication, either via the Replicator or manually by you.

The Replicator calls the server to replicate with a database replica on the server. The Replicator can also access a server via a passthru server connection, or a remote LAN server connection.

In addition to learning how to use the Replicator page, in this chapter you will learn how to create a local replica copy of a database on your workstation (and workspace), how to carry out selective replication (replicating only certain information), and how to replicate your mail database as well as other databases.

A Map of the Replicator

To guide you through setting Replicator options, here is a map with descriptions of all the buttons and icons on the Replicator page.

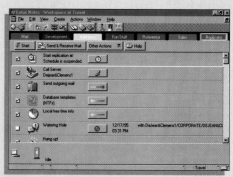

1 Each entry on the Replicator page has action buttons to use when setting replication options.

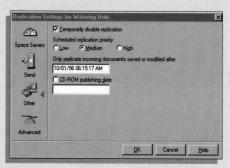

9 Select Other in the Replication Settings dialog box and then deselect the Temporarily Disable Replication option. Click on OK to close and save your selection.

8 This button (with the strikethrough icon) indicates that replication for this database has been disabled. To enable replication for the database, select the database on your workspace (or open it) and choose File, Replication, Settings.

2 The Clock button allows you to schedule replication times. Click on the button and the current Location document will open.

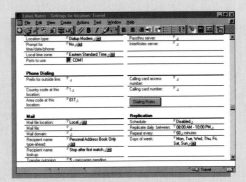

3 In the Location document, scroll down to the Replication section and enter Enable in the Schedule field. In addition, enter the times between which you want to replicate databases. In the Repeat Every field, enter the frequency of replication in minutes. In the Days Of Week field, enter the days you want to replicate databases. Save and close the document (press Esc).

4 You can click on the Phone button to call a different server than the one listed. Click on the Phone button to bring up the Call Server dialog box.

5 Select another server from the Call Server dialog box. Notes displays the server you have entered phone numbers for in the Server Connection documents in your address book. To add a server, choose File, Mobile, Server Phone Numbers. When you are finished selecting a server, click on OK.

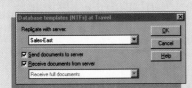

7 Under the Replicate With Server option, you can change the server the database is replicating with to any available server. You can send (replicate) documents to the server and/or receive documents from the server. When you receive documents from the server you can also select to receive the full documents, summaries, and/or the first 40K of rich text.

6 The arrow button allows you to choose the direction you want to replicate in. Click on the arrow button.

How to Create a Replicator Entry

Notes adds your local database entries to your Replicator when you first set up Notes; however, you can add, move, and delete entries to customize the Replicator to meet your own needs. You can create a Call entry or a Hangup entry to easily call a server or hang up a call.

▶ **1** To create a Call entry on the Replicator page, go to the Replicator and select where you want to place the Call entry. Notes will place the Call entry directly above your selection. Make sure the current location is one you use a dialup connection with to connect to a server.

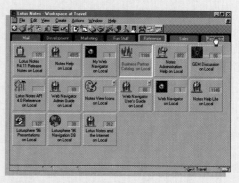

7 To add a Database entry to the Replicator page, the database icon must first be added to one of your workspace pages. Select the database icon on the workspace page and drag it to the Replicator tab until an outline forms around the tab. Let go of the icon and it will appear as a Database entry on the Replicator page.

TIP SHEET

▶ **You do not need a Call entry to a server for databases to replicate. When the Replicator reaches a Database entry, it will call the server on its own to begin replication.**

▶ **After the Replicator has called a server, it stays connected to the server until it reaches another Call entry, Database entry for a different server, or a Hangup entry. You can have two Call entries next to one another; however, once the Replicator connects to a server, it jumps to the next entry that is not a Call entry.**

▶ **You only need one Hangup entry at the end of the Replicator entries.**

▶ **You cannot move the Start Replication At entry in the Replicator because it must always be the first entry.**

2 Choose Create, Call Entry.

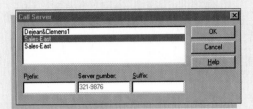

3 Notes creates the entry using your home server as the calling server. To change the server, click on the Call Entry button (it has a phone icon). From the Call Server dialog box, select the server you want to call and then click on OK.

4 To create a Hangup entry in the Replicator, on the Replicator page, select where you want the entry to go and choose Create, Hangup Entry.

6 You can delete Database, Call, and Hangup entries from the Replicator page. To delete an entry, select it and choose Edit, Clear, or press the Delete key.

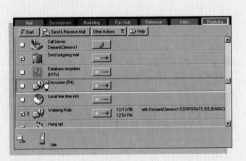

5 To move a Replicator entry to a higher or lower spot in the entry lineup, click on and then drag the entry to the position where you want it to go.

How to Replicate Databases Using the Replicator

The Replicator allows you to replicate your local databases in the background, and have replication occur automatically. Whether your current location is on a network or via modem, the Replicator replicates databases on one or more Notes servers. The Replicator can replicate all your entries, your mail file, one database, selected databases, and those databases designated as high priority databases.

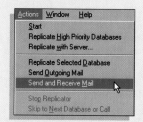

1 Using the Replicator, you can replicate your mail file in one of two ways. The first way is to go to the Replicator page and choose Actions, Send and Receive Mail. Alternatively, you can click on the Send & Receive Mail button on the Action bar.

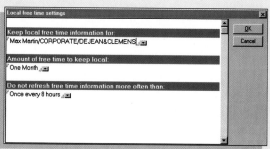

9 To select your free time settings for your Calendar, click on the arrow button on the Local Free Time entry. In the free time settings, enter the names of people you want to keep information for, the amount of free time to keep locally, and how often to refresh your free time information.

High-priority database

8 To replicate high priority databases from the Replicator page, choose Actions, Replicate High Priority Databases. High priority databases appear with a red exclamation mark in the left column of the Database entry.

TIP SHEET

▶ **To assign a database a high priority, select the Database entry, then click the right mouse button and choose Replication Settings. Alternatively, select the database's icon on the workspace page and choose File, Replication, Settings.**

▶ **To go to a database icon from a Database entry, double-click on the Database entry on the Replicator page.**

▶ **To stop replicating the current Database entry and go to the next one, click on the Next button on the bottom of the Replicator page.**

2 Another way to replicate your mail is to go to the toolbar and choose Actions, Send Outgoing Mail. This action will send outgoing mail from your MAIL.BOX database to your mail server, and then delete it from your local MAIL.BOX database. The mail you send while you are working remotely (at a mobile location) is saved in the MAIL.BOX database until you replicate your mail.

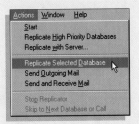

3 To replicate one database, select the Database entry on the Replicator page, and choose Actions, Replicate Selected Database.

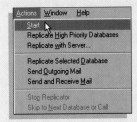

4 To replicate two or more selected databases, select the Database entries by placing a checkmark in the left column (small white box) of the Database entries. Make sure the entries you don't want to replicate do not have checkmarks. Once the entries are selected, choose Actions, Start, or click on the Start button on the Action bar.

5 To replicate all selected Replicator entries with a specific server, first select all the Database entries you want to replicate. Once the entries are selected, choose Actions, Replicate with Server.

7 To stop replication at any time, click on the Stop button on the bottom of the Replicator page. To follow the replication progress, look at the Progress bar as well as the server and workstation icons on the bottom of the Replicator page.

6 In the Replicate With Which Server? dialog box, select a server and then click on OK.

How to Replicate Databases in the Foreground

The advantage of using the Replicator to replicate databases is that replication can occur in the background while you continue to work in the foreground. You do have the choice of replicating a database in the foreground; however, you must initiate replication manually. This is useful in cases when you would otherwise not replicate a database, or when you want to watch the progress of the database replication closely.

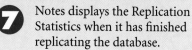

1 Select a local replica you want to replicate by selecting its database icon on a workspace page.

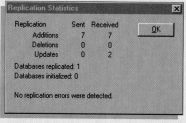

7 Notes displays the Replication Statistics when it has finished replicating the database.

TIP SHEET

▸ **You can replicate your local mail replica in the foreground the same way you replicate other local databases in the foreground.**

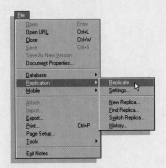

2 Choose File, Replication, Replicate.

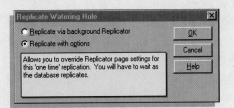

3 Select the Replicate With Options radio button and then click on OK.

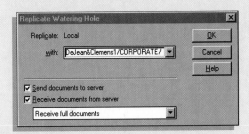

4 Select a server to replicate with if you want a different server than the one displayed.

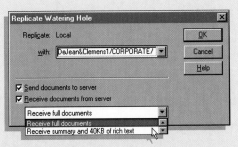

5 Select the Send Documents To Server option and/or the Receive Documents From Server option. In addition, under the Receive Documents From Server option, a pop-up menu is available, allowing you to receive document summaries with or without the first 40K of rich text.

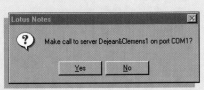

6 If you are using a mobile connection, Notes will ask you if you want to call the server. Select Yes. In the Call Server dialog box, click on the Auto Dial button. Notes will now dial the server and begin replicating the database.

How to Create a Local Replica

A replica is an identical copy of a database. Every replica of an original database shares the same replica ID as the original database. Notes recognizes databases as replicas of one another by the replica ID they have in common. By creating a replica on your local drive (hence, a local replica), you can store and update databases you read often, and offline (while not connected to a Notes server). You also have the option of creating a full or partial replica, so you can store a smaller version of a database.

▶ **1** To create your own replica of a database on your local drive, the database icon must first be added to your workspace. The icon you have added represents the replica on a server.

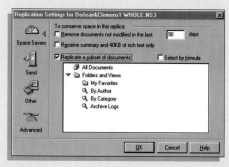

8 You can reduce the size of the replica by selecting some or all of the options in the Space Savers, Send, Other, and Advanced sections of the Replication Settings dialog box. For more details on how to use these options, see the next page in this chapter.

7 At this point you can click on OK to create the replica. If you want to create a partial replica (a smaller version of the original database), click on the Replication Settings button.

2 To create a full replica (which contains all documents and the design of the database), select the database icon you want to make a local replica of, and choose File, Replication, New Replica.

3 In the Server field of the New Replica dialog box, select Local. You can enter a new title in the Title field, or keep the title the same. You can also enter a new file name, or keep it the same.

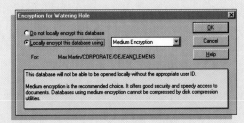

4 Optionally, you can encrypt the replica. Once encrypted, the local replica can only be opened by using your user ID. To encrypt the replica, click on the Encrypt button and select Locally Encrypt This Database. Then click on OK to close the dialog box.

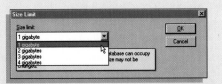

6 In the Create option, select Immediately. To create a full text index when the replica is created, click on the Create Full Text Index For Searching button. The Copy Access Control List option is selected by default. The ACL will not take effect while the replica is on a local drive, so it is not necessary to copy the ACL along with the replica. You can, however, keep this option selected and edit the ACL once the replica is created.

5 You can control the size that the replica can grow to by clicking on the Size Limit button. You can choose 1, 2, 3, or 4 gigabytes.

How to Access Replication Information and Settings

You can open a database's Properties infobox to view information about a database's replication settings, and you can customize those settings. The replication settings allow you to control what is stored in your local replicas and manage the range and kind of information you are replicating to your local replicas.

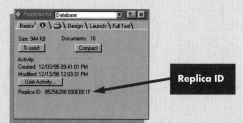

1 To see a database's replica ID, select or open the database and choose File, Database, Properties. Then select the Information tab in the Properties infobox.

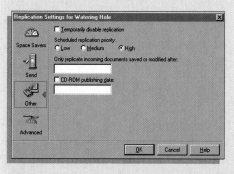

8 In the Other section, you can disable replication by selecting the Temporarily Disable Replication option. In addition, you can select the replication priority to receive only documents that were saved or modified after a date you specify. If you publish a database on a CD-ROM, you can specify a date for the database so that users can replicate with the database without having to carry out a full replication each time they access it.

2 Select the Basics tab of the database's Properties infobox, and then click on the Replication History button.

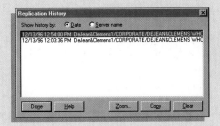

3 You can view the replication history of a database to see the servers the replica has replicated with as well as the dates of replication. You can copy and/or clear (delete) the history. You can also sort the history by date or by server.

4 To access replication settings for a replica, click on the Replication Settings button on the Basics tab in the Properties infobox.

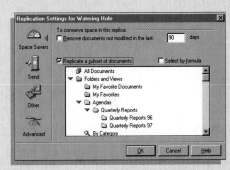

5 In the Space Savers section, if you want to purge documents that have not been modified in a specific amount of time, select the Remove Documents Not Modified In The Last option, then enter the number of days.

7 In the Send section there are three options you can select. Do Not Send Deletions Made In This Replica To Other Replicas, when selected, will not delete documents in another replica which you have deleted from your replica. Do Not Send Changes In Database Title & Catalog Info To Other Replicas, when selected, will not send changes you have made to your database title or catalog information to other replicas. Do Not Send Changes In Local Security Property To Other Replicas, when selected, will not change the local security settings in other replicas.

6 To replicate a portion of the documents in the database, select the Replicate A Subset Of Documents option, then select which folders and views you want to replicate documents from.

TRY IT!

In this last Try It! exercise you will create a personal agent that copies documents from one database to another. The agent will be scheduled to automatically run in the background on a daily basis. You will also create a search query for the agent so it can select documents that fit your criteria and then copy those documents to another database.

This example is going to use a mail database to create and store the agent, and documents will be copied to an archive database (which you may need to create). Remember that you must have sufficient access in both your mail database and the second database you are copying documents to, which means you need at least Author access to the second database (you are the Manager of your mail database). You can use your local mail database and another local database to complete this task. Both databases must be on the same Notes server (or workstation) for the scheduled agent to work, and you must select Enable Scheduled Local Agents in User Preferences.

Open your mail database and create a new agent.

Enter a name for the agent and choose to run it daily.

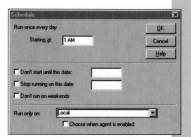

Schedule the agent to run at 1:00 A.M. every morning.

4

Do not run the agent on weekends. Choose to run the agent only on your workstation (Local).

7

Once the first query is saved to the agent, place the cursor after the first query and click on Add Search again to add the second query. In the example, the second query searches the Body field of each document to find the word "widget."

5

Run the agent on all documents in the database.

8

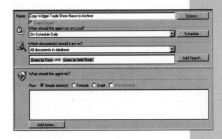

Notice two search queries are separated by *and* in the text box. You can change the *and* to *or* to include documents that match either search query. You can save the agent at any time by choosing File, Save.

6

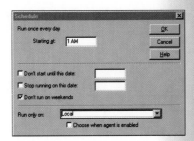

Add a search query to select documents that you want to copy to the second database. In this example, two queries are added to the agent. The first query finds all documents created with the Memo form that contain the phrase "Widget Trade Show" in the Subject or Body field.

9

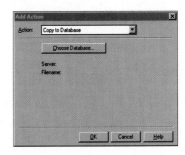

Select Simple Action(s) and then select an action that will copy the documents to a designated database.

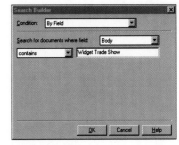

Continue to next page ▶

TRY IT!

Continue below

Select the options you want, then click on Specify Archive Location (on the Action bar) to specify the file name and location of the archive database. Select Locally to save the archive to your local drive, or select On Server to choose a server to save it to. Check with your Notes Administrator to ensure that there is adequate space available for your archive database. If you want to, change the name of the archive file in the Archive File text box. Once you have completed the Archive Profile, close and save it (you can use the Save Profile and Close buttons on the Action bar). Notes saves the profile to your mail database and creates an archive database.

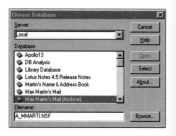

Choose a database to copy the documents to. In this example, the documents will be copied to an archive database. An archive of your mail database is created the first time you choose to archive mail. If you do not have an archive of your mail database, create one now by following the next two steps; otherwise skip to step 13.

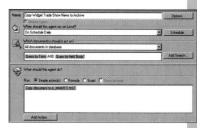

You should now have the agent completely filled out, including any search queries you want to use to select documents, and the action added to the design pane.

To create an archive database, open your mail database to the Archiving view and click on Setup Archive on the Action bar.

If you desire, you can add additional actions or search queries to the design pane. When you are done, save and close the agent.

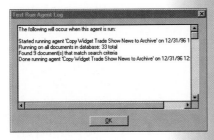

You can test
the agent to
make sure it
will do what
you want it
to. To do this,
first make a copy of the agent without
the actions in the design pane (so that
the agent does not act on documents).
Select the agent in the list of agents in the
database, then choose Actions, Test. The
Test Run Agent Log dialog box will appear telling you which actions the agent
performed. Alternatively, you can make a
copy of the database and run the agent in
the copy so that you protect your original copy of your mail database.

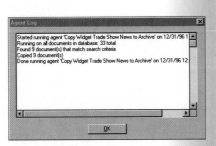

You can also
view the log
of an agent to
see what ac-
tivity it last
performed.
Open the database and choose View,
Agents. Select the agent and choose
Agent, Log. To view the agent's properties, choose Agent, Agent Properties.

CHAPTER 15

Printing

 Notes allows you to print a paper copy of a document, or a list of selected documents in a view or folder. Alternatively, you can print to a file that is saved on your local disk.

In this chapter we will show you how to print from a Notes database and set printer settings so that you can customize your printouts. You'll learn how to preview a document to see how it will appear when it's printed, attach headers and footers to your document, and adjust the margins of your printed copy.

How to Set Up Your Printer

In order to print in Notes, you must first make sure that your printer is turned on and that your workstation can communicate with the printer. You'll also need to make sure that your printer settings are correct. You'll need to specify a printer, a paper source (tray), and the size and scaling of the print job, as well as the way the printer will orient the print job (portrait or landscape).

► **1** Choose File, Print to open the File Print dialog box.

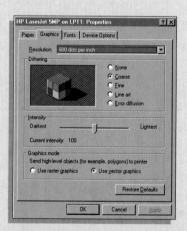

6 To access printer settings, such as printing of graphics, choose File, Print and select Printer. Click on the Setup button in Windows, or the Options button in UNIX. On the Macintosh, choose File, Page Setup.

TIP SHEET

▶ **Some print settings—such as print orientation (landscape or portrait), paper size, and scaling—are only available on some operating systems. If the option is available to you, Notes can spool a print job to your operating system's print spooler so that you can print to the background (when it is enabled).**

2 Click on the Printer button in the File Print dialog box. If you are working on a Macintosh, select a printer through the Chooser, which is located in the Apple menu.

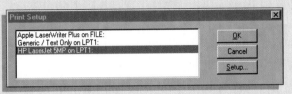

3 Notes displays the printers currently available to your workstation (the printers that have been installed in the Windows or OS/2 Control Panel). Select a printer and then click on the OK button. If you are working on a UNIX workstation, click on the Options button in the File Print dialog box and then select a printer under Printer Name.

4 To specify the orientation of your print job, choose File, Print, click on the Printer button, and then on the Setup button. Under Orientation, select either Portrait or Landscape. On the Macintosh, choose File, Page Setup, then select one of the orientation icons under Orientation. Landscape orientation is useful when you are printing a document that is wider than your printer can print on a single page of paper, such as a table that has several columns that will not fit on a single potrait-oriented printout. A portrait orientation is most often used for printing mail and other documents that fit on letter size paper.

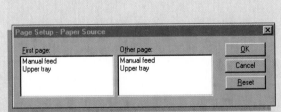

5 You can specify your paper source (which tray you are printing to), and the way you specify this setting depends on which operating system you are using. In Windows, choose File, Page Setup and select Paper. On the Macintosh, choose File, Print and select Options under Paper Source. In OS/2, choose File, Print, select Printer, and then Setup. In UNIX, choose File, Print, select Printer, and then select Options.

How to Prepare a Document for Printing

You can prepare a document(s) to print in a customized format. You can insert page breaks in the document, keep paragraphs from being split between pages, set print margins, add headers and/or footers, number pages, and crop pages.

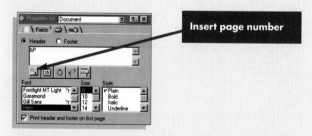

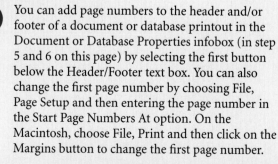

1 You can insert a page break to force a document to end printing a page at a specific line. To do this, open the document in edit mode and place the cursor where you want to insert the page break. Then choose Create, Page Break. The page break will be inserted above the current paragraph.

8 You can crop (reduce) the area of the page your job prints on. First choose File, Page Setup. In the text boxes under Page Size Cropping, enter the width and height of the area you want to print the job in, as measured from the upper left corner of the page. To do this on the Macintosh, choose File, Print and click on the Margins button.

Insert page number

7 You can add page numbers to the header and/or footer of a document or database printout in the Document or Database Properties infobox (in step 5 and 6 on this page) by selecting the first button below the Header/Footer text box. You can also change the first page number by choosing File, Page Setup and then entering the page number in the Start Page Numbers At option. On the Macintosh, choose File, Print and then click on the Margins button to change the first page number.

TIP SHEET

▸ **You can only insert page breaks in a rich text field.**

2 To view page breaks in a document, choose View, Show, Page Breaks.

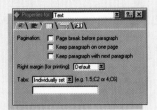

3 To keep all the lines of a paragraph on the same page, open the document in edit mode and place the cursor in the paragraph. Choose Text, Text Properties, select the Page tab, and then select the Keep Paragraph On One Page option. To keep consecutive paragraphs on the same page, select the Keep Paragraph With Next Paragraph option.

4 To set print margins for a print job, choose File, Page Setup (on the Macintosh, choose File, Print and then click on the Margins button). In the Margins section, enter the widths and heights in the respective text boxes in inches or centimeters (depending on which measurement system you have chosen in User Preferences).

5 You can enter header and/or footer information for a document or a database. To do so for a document, choose File, Document Properties and select the Printer tab. Select either Header or Footer and enter text. Note that you can use the icons below the text box to enter information.

6 To enter header and/or footer information for a database, choose File, Database Properties and select the Printer tab.

How to Preview and Print Documents

You can preview a document to review how its formatting will appear (for example, where page breaks will occur) before it is sent it to the printer. This is useful in many applications, including Notes, because documents don't always look the same on the screen as they do when they are printed. Be aware that Notes does not display headers and footers when previewing a document.

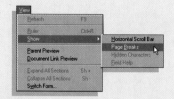

▶ **1** To preview a document, open it and choose View, Show, Page Breaks.

TIP SHEET

▶ **To print two or more documents, select the documents you want to print in the view pane. Choose File, Print and enter the selections for the print job, including number of pages, quality, number of copies of each document, and the graphics scaling. Under View Options, select Print Selected Documents and then click on OK to print the documents. (On the Macintosh, refer to the figure in step 6, and make sure that Selected documents is selected under Selection.)**

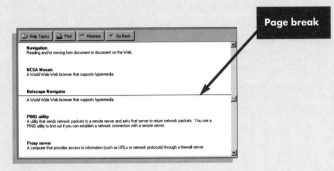

Page break

2 A page break appears as a solid line across the page.

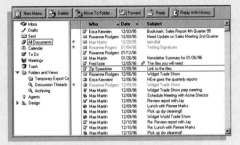

3 To print a document, open the document or select the document title in the view pane.

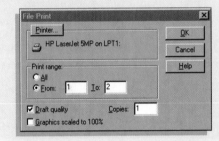

4 Choose File, Print. In the Print Range section, select the All radio button to print all the pages of the document. Otherwise, select the From radio button and then enter the starting page and the ending page, such as "1 to 4."

5 Select Draft Quality to print the document faster and with reduced quality. To print more than one copy, enter the number of copies in the Copies text box. Select Graphics Scaled To 100% to print graphics at their original size. Click on OK to print. To cancel the print job while it is in progress, click on the Cancel button in the Notes Message dialog box.

6 On the Macintosh, you can print by selecting File, Print. Enter the number of copies and the pages you want to print (all or a range) in the appropriate boxes, just as it was described in step 4. In addition, under Separate Documents By you can choose to separate document pages with a page break or an extra line, or choose no separation. Also make sure that Selected Documents is selected in the Selection option. Press Command+. (period) to stop a Macintosh print job.

How to Print a List of Documents in a Folder or View

You can print a list of documents as you see them in a folder or view in a database. You have the option of printing some of the docu-ments listed or all of them. In addition, you can print more than one copy and set the print quality, if you desire.

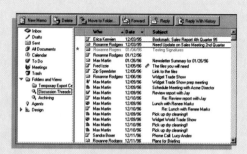

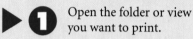

▶ **1** Open the folder or view you want to print.

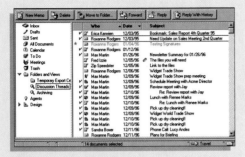

2 To print a list of only some of the documents in the folder or view, select those that you want to appear in the printout. Otherwise, the entire list of documents in the view or folder will be printed (as long as no documents are selected).

3 Choose File, Print.

4 Under Optional Settings, select the Draft Quality option for faster printing, and specify the number of copies you want to print.

5 Select Print View and then click on the OK button. Notes will tell you that it is sending the document to the printer.

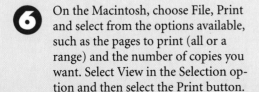

6 On the Macintosh, choose File, Print and select from the options available, such as the pages to print (all or a range) and the number of copies you want. Select View in the Selection option and then select the Print button.

How to Print to a File

You can print to a file instead of to the printer when you have a PostScript printer selected in your Printer Setup for your operating system. Printing to a file is slightly different on most operating systems, and we'll point out some of the differences here.

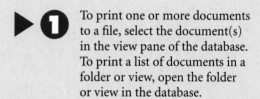

To print one or more documents to a file, select the document(s) in the view pane of the database. To print a list of documents in a folder or view, open the folder or view in the database.

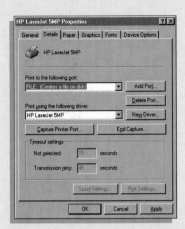

2 To prepare Windows 95 to print to a file, choose Settings, Printers from the Start menu and then select a printer. Next, choose File, Properties and select the Details tab. Under Print To The Following Port, select the File option and then click on OK.

3 Choose File, Print and choose either "All" selected documents, or print the view (or folder).

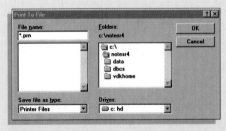

4 In Windows 3.x, select Setup, then Options, and then Encapsulated PostScript File. Enter a file name in the Print To File dialog box. In Windows 95, select the PostScript printer ending with "on FILE" and click on OK. Then enter a file name in the Print To File dialog box. In OS/2, select Setup, then Options, and then Raw PostScript File or Encapsulated PostScript File and enter a file name. In UNIX, select File, enter a file name and then select Apply. You can print a file to PostScript or PCL in UNIX.

5 On the Macintosh, choose File, Print and select PostScript File in Destination. Verify that the appropriate option is marked under Selection—either Selected Documents (for printing documents) or View (for printing a list from a view or folder). Click on the Save button and then enter a file name (and a location) to save the file.

How to Print Your Calendar and Use Form Override

In Notes you can print a list of your calendar entries. You have the option of printing either all of your calendar entries or calendar entries encompassing a specific range of dates.

When printing a selected document(s), you can use the form override feature, allowing you to print the document using one of the other forms available in the database. This is useful when you want to display a document with the form it was created in, and then print the document using a different form specially designed for printing.

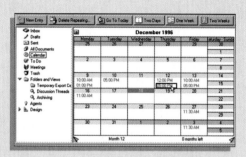

1 To print your calendar, open your mail database and select the Calendar view.

8 In the Print Form Override dialog box, select the form you want to print with and then click on OK. Click on OK in the File Print dialog box to print the selected document(s). The form override stays in effect only for that specific print job and will need to be selected each time a job is to be printed using a specific form other than the one used to display the document.

7 Choose File, Print, and select the Print Selected Documents radio button. Now click on the Form Override button.

2 Choose File, Print.

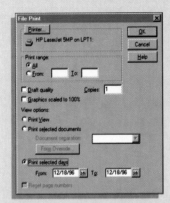

3 Select the Print Selected Days radio button and enter the range of days you want to print, including a start date (From) and an end date (To).

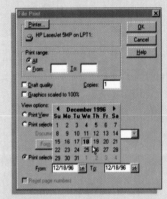

4 You can insert dates in these fields using the Calendar menu. Click on the calendar icon to make the menu pop up. When finished, click on the OK button to print the calendar dates.

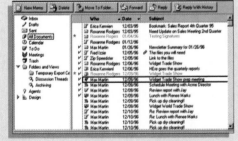

6 To print a document(s) with a different form than the form used to display the document, select the document(s) you want to print in the view pane.

5 On the Macintosh, choose File, Print and select View from the Selection option. Under Pages, select the All option to print all calendar entries, or enter a range of dates in the From and To text boxes. Click on Print to print the calendar dates.

CHAPTER 16

Searching Notes Databases

 Notes allows you to search for and find information contained in one document, selected documents, an entire database, or several databases at once. Also, when a database is full text indexed, you can carry out more complex and criteria-dependent searches.

This chapter covers how to use the Find and Find/Replace options, which allow you to search out and edit text in a document. When you are in a document in read mode, you can search for text, and you can specify Find options to search by whole word, case, and/or accent. When you are in a document in edit mode, you can search for text and replace it. You can also use the find and replace feature on document titles in a view.

This chapter will also show you how to make the most of full text searching your Notes databases. The full text search feature is accessible by displaying the Search bar at the top of the Notes window. The Search bar will assist you in formulating searches in a database. You can build a search formula for documents that contain a specific word, phrase, or one or more words in a list. You can also search for documents that have been created by a specific author, created or modified on a specific date or range of dates, and documents that contain data in a particular field. In addition, you can search for documents created with a specific form and look at documents that meet specific criteria or do not contain specific information.

You can refine, reset, and save searches. You can control how search results are displayed, limit the scope of searches, and search formulas in the Search bar or by using a search builder to construct search formulas. Full text searching is a powerful Notes database feature, both for finding information quickly and easily, and for referring to information later on.

How to Find and Replace Text in a Document

You can search for text in a document when it is open in read mode. In edit mode, you can both search for and replace text. You can also search for text in document titles in a view. Here's how to do these things.

1 To search a document, open in read mode, choose Edit, Find/Replace. This dialog box will appear.

7 Click on Find Next to search down the document, or Find Previous to search up the document. When Notes finds an instance of your text, you can select Replace to replace the highlighted text, select Replace All to replace all instances of your text, or select Find Next or Find Previous to move on to the next instance without changing the highlighted text. When you are finished searching and replacing text, click on Done.

▶ **To search for text in document titles in a view, open the view and select Edit, Find/Replace. Enter the word or phrase you want to find in the Find text box. Click on Find Next to search for occurrences of the text in documents listed after the one you have selected in the view. Click on Find Previous to search for occurrences of the text in documents listed before the one you have selected in the view.**

2 Enter the word or phrase you want to search for in the Find text box. Notice that the Replace text box is grayed out—you cannot edit a document in read mode. Under Match, select Whole Word to find the text you have typed with spaces around it (representing the individual word). Select Accent to match the accented characters in the text you have typed. Select Case to match the exact case of the text you have typed.

3 Click on Find Next to search down the document, or Find Previous to search up the document. Notes will search all fields containing text.

4 To find and replace text in a document, open the document in edit mode and choose Edit, Find/Replace.

5 Enter the word or phrase you want to find in the Find text box. If you want to replace found text with other text, enter the replacement text in the Replace text box.

6 Under Match, select Whole Word to find the text you have typed with spaces around it (representing the individual word). Select Accent to match the accented characters in the text you have typed. Select Case to match the exact case of the text you have typed.

How to Enter Text in the Search Bar

You can use the Search bar to search for text in a database, whether or not the database is full text indexed. The Search bar appears at the top of the Notes window. When you enter a search in the Search bar text box, Notes will search all the documents in the current view. Make sure that the view you want to search in is open.

▶ **1** To open the Search bar, choose View, Search Bar.

8 Depending on the browser you have chosen to use in your Current Location document, Notes will either open the Web page in a Notes window or another Web browser. The figure here shows Notes opening the Lotus home page in a Notes window on a Macintosh. To change how Notes displays Web pages, you must edit your Current Location document. Choose File, Mobile, Edit Current Location.

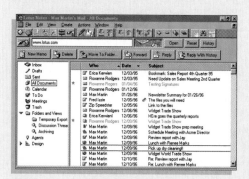

7 You can open a Web page from the Search bar in any database (including the Personal and Server Web Navigator databases). To do this, open a database and choose View, Search Bar. Select the icon to the left of the Search bar to display the Open URL icon. Enter the URL of the Web page you want to open and click on the Open button.

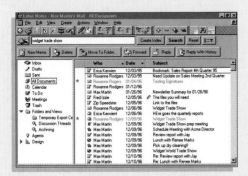

2 If you want to search documents in a database that is not full text indexed, enter the text you want to find in the Search bar text box.

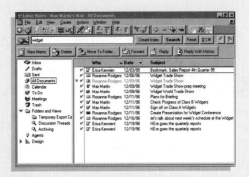

3 Select the Search button on the Search bar. Notes displays only documents that contain the text you are searching for.

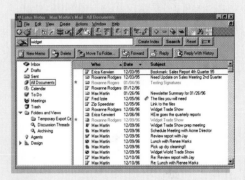

4 To view all the documents in the view again (not just the documents found in the search), click on the Reset button. Click on Reset again to clear the Search bar text box.

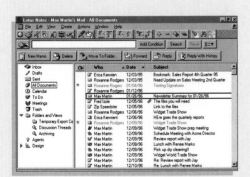

6 When a database is full text indexed, the Add Condition button appears on the Search bar. You can enter a word or phrase (or search formula) into the Search bar text box, or you can click on the Add Condition button to use the Search Builder to add a search formula to the Search bar.

5 To search a database that has been full text indexed, choose View, Search Bar to display the Search bar. To determine if a database has been full text indexed, choose File, Database, Properties, and select the Full Text tab. If the database does not have an index it will say so. Otherwise, index information and current settings appear on this tab. To learn how to index a database, refer to the next page in this chapter, "How to Create a Full Text Index for a Database."

How to Create a Full Text Index for a Database

When you create a full text index for a database you can create more complex searches. Here's how to create and manage full text indexes for local- and server-based databases. Keep in mind that when a database resides on a server, you must have at least Designer access in the database's ACL to create and update the full text index.

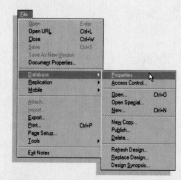

▶ **1** To full text index a database, open the database and choose File, Database, Properties.

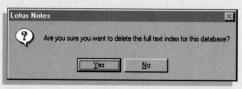

8 To delete a database's full text index, click on the Delete Index button. You will be asked to confirm that you want to delete the index.

7 If the database resides on a server, you can specify how frequently the index is updated in the Update Frequency (Servers Only) option. Select the pop-up menu and choose Daily, Scheduled, Hourly, or Immediately.

▶ **Full text indexes do not replicate with the database. You must create a full text index for each replica of a database, however, the full text index options for the replica are applied to new replicas of the database.**

▶ **Keep in mind that selecting the Index Encrypted Fields option will compromise the security of encrypted field data.**

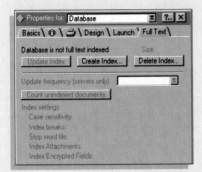

2 In the Database Properties infobox, click on Create Index.

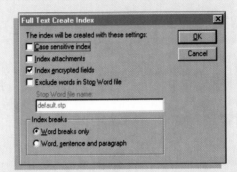

3 Select the settings for the full text index from the Full Text Create Index dialog box. The Case Sensitive Index option indexes a word for each case occurrence. The Index Attachments option indexes text in file attachments. The Index Encrypted Fields option indexes encrypted fields. The Exclude Words In Stop Word File option allows you to create a file to add words that are not indexed. In the Index Breaks section, you can select Word Breaks Only to search for just that, or select Word, Sentence, And Paragraph Breaks, to use proximity operators when searching for the proximity of two words. Keep in mind that by selecting options other than the default options set in this dialog box, you will create a larger full text index.

4 Once you have chosen settings in the Full Text Create Index dialog box, click on the OK button to begin creating the index. If you have the Enable Local Background Indexing option selected in your User Preferences, the index will be created in the background while you continue working. Otherwise, the index will be created in the foreground.

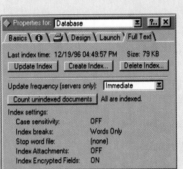

6 To update the full text index manually, click on the Update Index button. If you have the Enable Local Background Indexing option selected in your User Preferences, every time you start Notes the program will update your full text indexed databases. To determine if a database has unindexed documents (needs updating), click on the Count Unindexed Documents button in the Database Properties infobox on the Full Text tab.

5 When a database is full text indexed, the Database Properties infobox looks like this one.

How to Use the Search Builder to Create Search Formulas

You can use the Search Builder dialog box when a Notes database is full text indexed. The Search Builder provides easy-to-use menus and text boxes that enable you to build complex search formulas that can be automatically inserted into the Search bar. On the next page you will learn how to refine and save your searches.

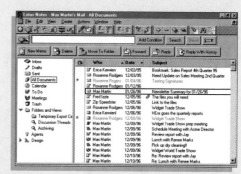

▶ **1** To search for documents in a database that contain a specific word or phrase, open the database to the view you want to search in and click on the Add Condition button.

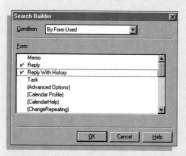

8 To search for documents in a database by the specific form used, open the database to the view you want to search in and click on the Add Condition button. Under Condition, select By Form Used. Under Form, select one or more forms by clicking once on the form name(s). A check mark appears next to each form selected.

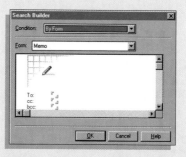

7 To search for documents in a database by form, open the database to the view you want to search in and click on the Add Condition button. Under Condition, select By Form. Select one of the forms in the database from the Form option. The form you choose appears below this option containing all the editable fields you can use to enter search text. Scroll down the form to enter text in fields not readily visible.

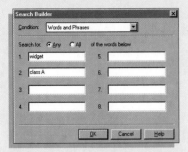

2 In the Condition option, select Words And Phrases. In the Search For option choose either to find any of the words or all of the words (in the latter case, the document must contain all the words and phrases you enter). In the text boxes numbered 1 through 8, enter the words and/or phrases you want to find.

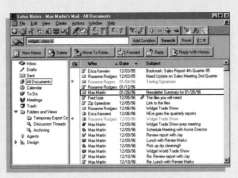

3 When you have finished entering the search words and phrases, click on the OK button. The search now appears in the Search bar. Click on Search to carry out the search.

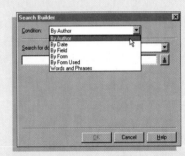

4 To search for documents in a database by author, open the database to the view you want to search in and click on the Add Condition button. Under Condition, select By Author.

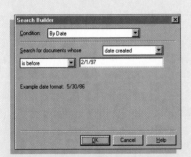

6 To search for documents in a database by date, open the database to the view you want to search in and click on the Add Condition button. Under Condition, select By Date. In the Search For Documents Whose option, enter either Date Created or Date Modified. Directly below this option, enter the criteria for the date, such as Is Before or Is Between. In the text box to the right of this option, enter the date.

5 Under the Search For Documents Whose Author option, select either Contains or Does Not Contain. Below this option, enter the name of the author whose documents you want to find. You can click on the Author icon to use your address book(s) to find and enter the author's name.

How to Refine and Save Your Searches

Now that you know how to enter search formulas using the Search Builder, let's look at some ways you can refine your searches. You can add search criteria, make a search case-sensitive, add variations and synonyms of a word to a search, adjust the relevance ranking of search words, and search by the proximity of words to one another. In addition, you can save your searches in the database, whether or not the database has been full text indexed.

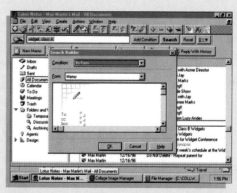

▶ **❶** Once you have entered a search with the Search Builder and the search appears in the Search bar, you can add criteria to the search. To do this, place the cursor after the last search formula in the Search bar and select Add Condition. For example, you may want to search for words/phrases by a specific form used. You would first enter the search by words and phrases, and then enter the second search formula for searching by form.

▶ **You can edit a search formula in the Search bar either by double-clicking on the search formula in the text box or by selecting the formula and then Add Condition.**

▶ **You can use wildcard characters in your text searches. Use a ? (question mark) for a single characters, and an * (asterisk) for multiple characters. Wildcard characters only work in fields that have text only (no numbers or dates).**

▶ **When the database searched is full text indexed, a red rectangle appears around a query match (in a document). A green rectangle appears around a match as you move to the match. You can move around the matches in a document by pressing Ctrl and + (plus key) to go forward, or Ctrl and - (minus key) to go backward. On the Macintosh, press Command and + or Command and -.**

❾ To clear the search results from the Search bar, click twice on the Reset button on the Search bar. On the first click, Notes clears the results of the search (the found documents), and on the second click Notes clears the search formula.

❽ When your database is full text indexed, you can adjust the way the search results are displayed. You can sort the results by relevance (when you have used relevance ranking in the search), by oldest first (oldest documents created or modified), or by newest first (most recently created or modified documents). To select a sorting option, select the Options menu at the end of the Search bar. You can also limit the maximum number of documents returned by a search by selecting Maximum Results from the Options menu.

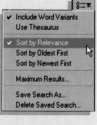

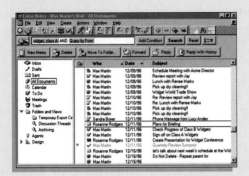

2 The Search bar now contains both search formulas for words and phrases and the form query. You can also remove an individual formula by selecting it and choosing Edit, Cut. You can paste it back into the Search bar by choosing Edit, Paste.

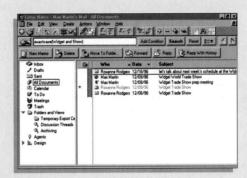

3 To create case-sensitive searches, use the Exactcase operator in front of your search text. For example, "Exactcase (Widget and Ace)" will find "Widget" and "Acme." "Exactcase Widget and Acme" will find "Widget" and "acme" or "Acme."

4 Notes automatically includes variations of words, such as "run," "running," and "runs," in text searches. You can choose to exclude words variants for a text search by deselecting Include Word Variants in the Options menu at the end of the Search bar.

5 You can use the Thesaurus to search for synonyms of words in your search. To do this, click the Options button on the Search bar and choose Use Thesaurus.

7 To use the Termweight operator, place the word *termweight* in front of the search word. The usage is as follows: termweight 80 *word1* or termweight 20 *word2*. For example, "termweight 75 Widget or termweight 25 Acme" will return documents that contain a greater occurrence of the word Widget than of the word Acme. The number following termweight can be between 0 and 100.

6 When your database is full text indexed, you can use the Termweight operator to set the relevance ranking of search words. When Notes displays the result of a search, it lists documents in order of relevance in the returned documents. In this figure,

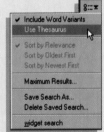

notice that the gray bar in the left column in the view pane is darker for the first few documents and then becomes lighter for the remaining documents. The documents most relevant to the search appear at the top of the results, in the darker portion of the gray bar.

How to Search in Multiple Databases

You can search more than one database at a time, and you can open more than one database in the navigation pane and search the view of each database in the same window. When your Notes administrator has set up one or more search site databases for server-based databases, you can search two or more databases (on Notes servers) at the same time. You can also create a search site database for your local databases so you can search two or more local databases at the same time.

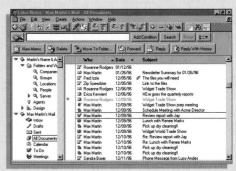

1 To open up two or more databases in one Notes window and search each one individually in the same window, open the Notes workspace and select the databases you want to open by holding down the Shift key and clicking on each database icon. While still holding down on the Shift key, double-click one of the database icons to open all of them in one window.

2 To carry out the search, first make sure the full text index for your search database has been created and/or updated. To do this, select the search site database icon on the workspace, choose the Full Text tab and select either Create Index or Update Index. Also, make sure that once the index has been updated, you go back to the search form in the search site database and select Start Search. Your search results appear in the order you requested (by relevance is the default).

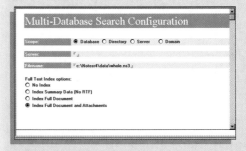

8 Under Scope, create a search scope configuration document for a database by selecting Database, or a directory on your local drive by selecting Directory. Do not select Server or Domain when creating a local search site database. Leave the Server field blank. In Filename, enter the full path and file name of the database or directory you want to add. When you enter a directory, Notes will add all the databases in the directory. An example of a directory path is "c:\Notes\Data."

You can now select a view from one of the databases in the navigation pane, and then click on the Add Condition button to enter a search formula. This is useful when you want to search databases consecutively without leaving the window of each database to go to the next database window and carry out another search.

To search multiple databases using a search site database, find out the location of a search site database from a Notes administrator, add the database to your workspace, and open it. You may also need the administrator to create Search Scope documents for the databases you want to search if they have not already been created.

When you open the search site database, a Search form appears. You can enter words to search for in the text box below Search For The Following Word(s). You can limit your search and control how search results are sorted by selecting the Options button to the right of the text box. Select Simple Search to find documents containing a word or phrase. To hide the options, click on the Options button again. To complete the search, select Start Search.

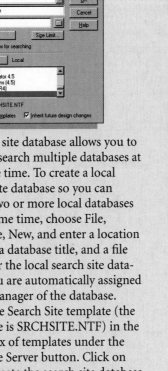

A search site database allows you to full text search multiple databases at the same time. To create a local search site database so you can search two or more local databases at the same time, choose File, Database, New, and enter a location (Local), a database title, and a file name for the local search site database. You are automatically assigned as the Manager of the database. Select the Search Site template (the file name is SRCHSITE.NTF) in the scroll box of templates under the Template Server button. Click on OK to create the search site database on your local drive.

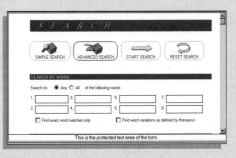

Select Advanced Search to find documents by specific criteria. Scroll down the document to view and enter any and all criteria you would like to base the search on. You can save an advanced search by scrolling to the bottom of the document and selecting Save Search. To complete the advanced search, select Start Search.

To add a database(s) to the search site database, open your local search site database and choose Create, Search Scope Configuration.

CHAPTER 17

Creating Agents

You can create automated tasks, called *agents,* in a Notes database. Agents can carry out several tasks in one step, allowing you to work more efficiently and save time. An agent comprises a selection formula, a trigger (a way to initiate running the agent), and one or more actions to perform. Notes databases support both personal and shared agents; however, to create shared agents in a database on a Notes server you must have at least Designer access to the database.

This chapter will show you how to create a personal agent in two ways: either by copying and pasting it or by creating it from scratch. You can name, rename, and assign specific actions to an agent. You can run an agent manually, schedule it to run automatically, run it when a document is pasted into a database, or run it when the database receives mail. You can limit the documents an agent processes and even add a search query to an agent. You can also run some agents from the workspace. An agent can modify documents, create new documents, or select documents in a view.

Both personal and private agents are stored in the database they were created in and can be accessed while the database is active. In this chapter you will see how personal agents are created in local databases. Note that when you have the appropriate access to databases on a server, shared agents are created the same way.

How to Create an Agent from Another Agent

You can create an agent in a database by copying one from the same database, or by taking it from another database. Once copied, you can then modify the agent. You can create and copy personal agents when you have at least Reader access to a database and have the Create Personal Agents option selected in the database's ACL. You can create and copy shared agents if you have at least Designer access to a database. On this page we'll show you how to create an agent by copying another agent, and on the next page we'll show you how to create an agent from scratch.

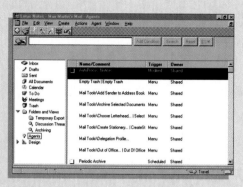

▶ ❶ To create an agent by copying one in the same database, first open the database and select Agents in the navigation pane, or choose View, Agents.

2 The list of agents in the database appears in the view pane. Select the agent you want to copy, then choose Edit, Copy.

3 Now choose Edit, Paste to create a new copy of the agent.

4 The newly copied agent appears with the name of the old agent prefixed with the words "Copy Of." Double-click on the new agent to rename it and/or modify it. For details on how to modify an agent, see the next page.

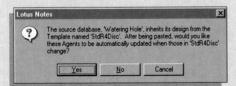

6 Now open the database you want to copy the agent to, choose View, Agents, then choose Edit, Paste. If you copy an agent from a database that is a design template, you will be asked if you want to keep the agent's design the same as the original database. Click on Yes if you want to keep the two agents identical, or click on No if you want to modify the agent. Double-click on the new copy of the agent to rename it and/or modify it.

5 To create an agent by copying an agent from another database, open the database that contains the agent you want to copy, then choose View, Agents. Select the agent you want to copy from the list of agents in the view pane, then choose Edit, Copy to copy the agent to the clipboard.

How to Create an Agent from Scratch

You can create an agent from scratch when you want to start with an untitled agent, or when you cannot find an existing agent that resembles the agent you want to create. Sometimes creating an agent from scratch is easier than working with a copy because you do not have to alter settings—you just have to add settings. If you have already begun to work with a copy of an agent, the steps on this page will help you complete modifications to the agent so that it works just the way you want it to.

▶ **1** To create an agent from scratch, open the database and choose Create, Agent.

 7 Close the agent by pressing Esc, then select Yes to save the agent.

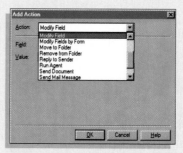

6 Click on the Add Action button to choose from a list of actions. In the Add Action option, select an option from the pop-up menu. Fill out any remaining options based on the action you have chosen under the Action option. For more details on assigning actions to an agent, see the next page. When you are done, click on OK.

TIP SHEET

▶ In the design pane, under What Should This Agent Do?, instead of selecting Simple Action(s), you can select Formula if you want to enter a formula using Notes formula language, or you can select Script if you want to enter a script using the LotusScript language. This requires knowledge of the Notes formula or LotusScript language, which is beyond the scope of the book. Learning the Notes formula language and/or LotusScript is covered under learning how to design Notes databases.

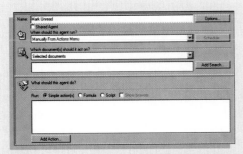

2 Enter a name for the agent in the Name text box. See the next page for some important details about naming an agent. Do not select Shared Agent because you are creating a personal agent.

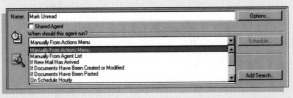

3 Under When Should This Agent Run?, select an option from the pop-up menu. The agent can run in a variety of ways: when you choose it manually from the Actions menu, when you choose it from the Agent list, when new mail arrives in the database, when documents are created or modified, when documents are pasted into the database, or on a schedule in the background.

4 Under Which Document(s) Should It Act On?, select an option from the pop-up menu. The agent can act on all documents in the database, all new and modified documents since the agent was last run, all unread documents in the current view, and selected documents in the current view, or it can run once using @Commands. @Commands are used with the Notes formula language (not covered in this book, but covered in Notes database design references).

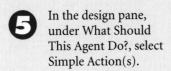

5 In the design pane, under What Should This Agent Do?, select Simple Action(s).

How to Name and Assign Actions to an Agent

On this page we'll show you some helpful hints and techniques that you can use when naming agents so they appear as you want them to in the Actions menu or in the Agents list in the database. You'll also see how to assign actions to an agent so that you can control what the agent is doing and how it is modifying documents in the database.

▶ ❶ To name or rename an agent, open the database, choose View, Agents, and double-click on the agent you want to rename. If you are naming an agent while creating it, the agent will already be open.

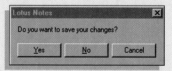

❼ When you have completed assigning the action(s) to the agent, make sure you have also filled out any remaining options for the agent. Close the agent by pressing Esc and click Yes to save the agent.

TIP SHEET

▸ **You can create a cascading menu to group similar agents together when they appear in the Actions menu. Do this by placing the top menu choice first, then a back-slash (\\), and then the specific agent name. For example, in your mail database, the Actions menu displays the Mail Tools menu which cascades to display the mail agents. The name of the agent for choosing a letterhead is "Mail Tools\\Choose Letterhead."**

▸ **You can also number the agents to have them appear in order in the Actions menu. For example, the name of the first agent might be "1. Choose Letterhead," and the second might be "2. Create Stationary," and so on.**

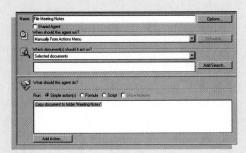

2 Enter or change the name of the agent in the Name text box.

3 You can assign an action, or a series of actions, for an agent to perform. The actions are accessible by opening the agent and choosing Simple Action(s) and in design pane. Select Add Action at the bottom of the design pane, then scroll through the available actions in the Actions menu in the resulting dialog box. Actions range from copying documents to folders and databases, to sending and replying to mail. In this example, the action is to copy documents to a folder, and the selected folder is "Meeting Notes."

4 Once the action is designated in the Add Action dialog box, click on OK to add the action to the design pane. The action appears as a gray box in the design pane, as pointed out here.

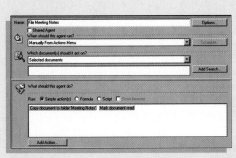

6 To add an additional action to the design pane, place the cursor after the last action (or after any action you want the new action to follow), and click on the Add Action button. Assign action attributes the same way you did for the previous actions. When you have created the new action and closed the Add Action dialog box, the new action will appear in the design pane, as in this example, where the two actions are to copy the document to the Meetings Notes folder and then mark the document as read.

5 To edit an action, double-click on the action or select the action's gray box and click on the Edit Action button.

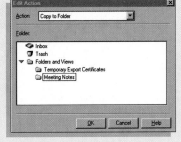

How to Run an Agent

There are several ways to run an agent, and the way you run the agent depends on what the agent is doing and in what location it is carrying out its tasks (for example, from a specific view or from the workspace). You can set up an agent to run in the following ways: manually when you select it from the Actions menu, as a hidden agent, on a schedule in the background, when there are new or modified documents, when the database receives mail, or when documents are pasted into the database.

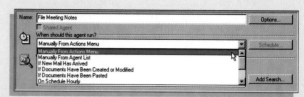

▶ **1** A manually run agent runs when it is selected from the Actions menu. To make an agent run manually, open the database and choose View, Agents. From the list of agents, double-click on an agent and under the When Should This Agent Run? option, select Manually From Actions Menu.

9 To create an agent that runs automatically when documents are pasted into the database, open the agent, and from the When Should This Agent Run? option select If Documents Have Been Pasted.

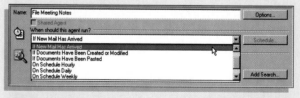

8 To create an agent that runs automatically when documents are mailed to the database, open the agent and from the When Should This Agent Run? option, select If New Mail Has Arrived.

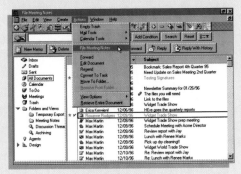

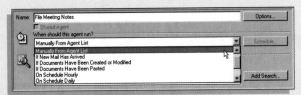

2 To run an agent manually, the agent's database must be selected or open. In this example, the agent acts on selected documents, so there must be documents selected in a view of the database. Once you have selected one or more documents, choose the agent from the Actions menu.

3 A hidden agent does not appear in the Actions menu, and instead must be run from the Agent window (the list of agents in the view pane). To make an agent hidden, open the agent, and from the When Should This Agent Run? option select Manually From Agent List.

4 To run a hidden agent, first open the database and choose View, Agents. Then select the agent and choose Actions, Run.

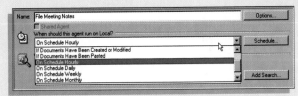

5 A scheduled agent runs in the background automatically. To run an agent on a schedule in the background, you must first designate when the agent will be run by Notes. Open the agent, and from the When Should This Agent Run? option select to run the agent hourly, daily, weekly, or monthly.

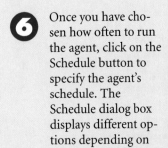

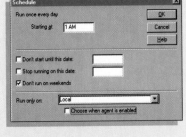

6 Once you have chosen how often to run the agent, click on the Schedule button to specify the agent's schedule. The Schedule dialog box displays different options depending on whether you choose hourly, daily, weekly, or monthly.

7 You can automatically run an agent on documents that are new or have been modified since the last time the agent was run. Open the agent and from the When Should This Agent Run? option, select If Documents Have Been Created Or Modified.

How to Build a Search Query for an Agent

You can make an agent to select documents to act on by adding a search query to the agent. The agent uses the Search Builder dialog box, which is the same as the Search Builder used when full-text searching a database. You can build a search query to select documents by author, by date, by one or more field values, by a certain form, by documents found in a specific folder or view, or by specific words and phrases.

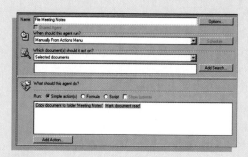

1 To build a search query for an agent, open the agent and click on the Add Search button.

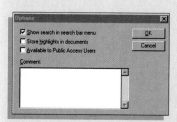

8 You can save a search query created in an agent so that it will be accessible from the full-text Search bar. Open the agent and click on the Options button in the top right corner. Select Show Search In Search Bar Menu to display the search query in the Search bar when the agent is run. Then the search can be saved using the Save Search As option on the Search bar. Select Store Highlights In Documents to save the red highlights around words found from the search query. Though this will increase your database's size, it will save time when running the agent query again.

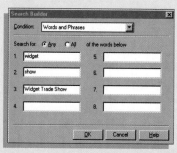

7 To build a search query that selects documents which contain words and phrases you specify, select Words and Phrases from the Condition option. In the Search For option, select either Any or All to find any or all of the words and phrases you list in the below text boxes. Enter words and/or phrases in the text boxes numbered one through eight.

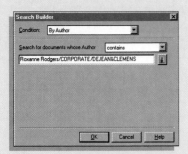

2 To select documents by the document's author (or *not* by a certain author), select By Author from the Condition option. In the Search For Documents Whose Author option, choose either Contains or Does Not Contain. In the text box at the bottom, enter the name of the author, or choose the name from the Name dialog box by clicking on the person icon to the right of the text box.

3 To build a search query that selects documents by creation or modification date, select By Date from the Condition option. In the Search For Documents Whose option, select either Date Modified or Date Created. Below that, select an option from the pop-up menu on the left, then enter the date in the text box to the right.

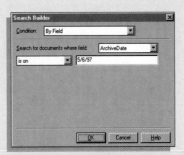

4 To build a search query that selects documents by the contents of a field, select By Field from the Condition option. In the Search For Documents Where Field option, select a field from the pop-up list of fields in the database. Complete the query by selecting a option in the bottom left box and then entering the search text in the text box on the bottom right.

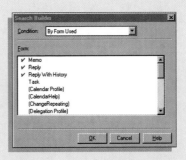

6 To build a search query that selects documents found in a specific folder or view, select By Folder from the Condition option. Under Folder, select a folder or view.

5 To build a search query that selects documents displayed using a specific form(s), select By Form Used from the Condition option. Under Form, select one or more forms by clicking on the form name(s). A checkmark will be placed next to the form.

How to Create an Agent That Sends Messages

You can create an agent that responds to mail, forwards a document, or sends a newsletter summary. All of these tasks can be entered in an agent using simple actions. Here's how.

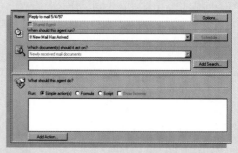

▶ **1** To create an agent that responds to mail, open the agent or create the agent by choosing Create, Agent. Enter a name for the agent in the Name text box, and select when the agent should run and which documents the agent should run on.

8 To create an agent that sends a document, open the agent or create the agent by choosing Create, Agent, and select when the agent should run and which documents the agent should run on. In the design pane, select Simple Action(s) and click the Add Action button. Select Send Document from the Action option.

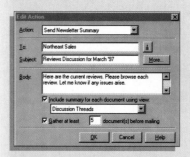

7 Enter the name of the recipient(s) in the To field, and the subject in the Subject field. To fill out CC and BCC fields, click the More button. Enter any additional text you want to add to the forwarded document in the Body field. Select the Include Summary For Each Document Using View option, then in the below pop-up menu, select a view to copy view information from (the view columns) to include in the summary for each link.

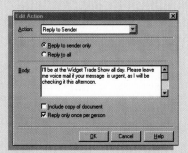

2 Go to the design pane, select Simple Action(s), then click the Add Action button. Select Reply To Sender in the Action option. Below that, select either the Reply To Sender Only or Reply To All radio button. Enter a message in the Body text box scrolling down if necessary. Be aware that this text box only accepts plain text.

3 Select Include Copy Of Document to add the original message to the end of your reply message. Select Reply Only Once Per Person to avoid sending more than one reply to the same person.

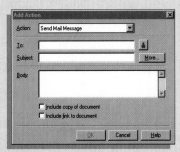

4 To create an agent that forwards mail, open the agent or create the agent by choosing Create, Agent, and select when the agent should run and which documents the agent should run on. In the design pane, select Simple Action(s) and click the Add Action button. Select Send Mail Message from the Action option.

6 A newsletter summary is one document containing several links to other related documents. To create an agent that sends a newsletter summary, open the agent or create the agent by choosing Create, Agent, and select when the agent should run and which documents the agent should run on. In the design pane, select Simple Action(s), and click the Add Action button. Select Send Newsletter Summary from the Action option.

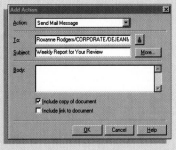

5 Enter the name of the recipient(s) in the To field, and the subject in the Subject field. To fill out CC and BCC fields, click the More button. Enter any additional text you want to add to the forwarded document in the Body field and select Include Copy Of Document.

CHAPTER 18

Securing Your Notes Desktop

 Notes offers a number of security options to protect against unauthorized access to your workstation, your local databases, and data contained in documents. One such feature is your user ID. Every Notes user has a unique user ID, which can be obtained from a Notes administrator, and/or can be stored in your Person document in a Public Name and Address Book. Likewise, Notes servers also have unique IDs.

Your user ID can be password-protected to prevent others from using your ID to access databases on Notes servers. You can set, change, or clear your password at any time directly from your Notes workstation, as long as you know your user ID. You can request to add certificates to your password and change your user ID owner name.

For further protection, you can encrypt databases and documents using encryption features in Notes. By encrypting data in fields in a document, you limit who can read and access data so that only users who have an encryption key can access encrypted fields in a document. You can use your user ID to encrypt local databases so that they cannot be accessed by another user at your workstation.

How to Set and Change Your Password

Your user ID is a file that has the file extension "ID." It uniquely identifies you as a user when you access your local workstation or a Notes server. It is recommended that you set a password for your user ID, and change it often (every two months or so). You can set, change, and clear your user ID password. Your user ID contains one or more certificates that you have in common with one or more Notes servers. When you have a certificate in common with a Notes server, the server grants you access to it.

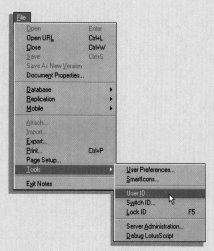

▶ **1** To set or change your password, choose File, Tools, User ID.

9 Enter your password in the text box and click on OK. Your password is now cleared.

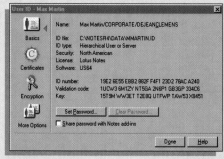

8 Click on the Clear Password button. You will not be able to clear your password if your Notes administrator requires you to enter a password for your user ID (the Clear Password button will be grayed out).

TIP SHEET

▶ **Notes passwords are case-sensitive, so make sure to enter the exact case for your password. For example, "JuliusCaesar123" is not the same as "juliuscaesar123."**

▶ **Passwords can be any combination of keyboard characters and numbers; however, the first character must be an alphanumeric character. The longer the password the more difficult it is to crack.**

▶ **Unlike passwords used on many network operating systems, the Notes user ID password can not be reset by an administrator in the background. When you change the password, it is only stored in the ID file. If you forget your password, your user ID must be replaced with a different copy which contains a known password. Notes Administrators normally keep a secured copy of each ID file containing a known password as a backup.**

2 Notes asks you to enter your password (if one exists). Enter it and click OK.

3 The User ID dialog box appears. Click on the Set Password button.

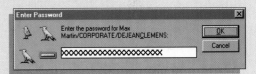

4 Enter the password for your user ID. If your user ID does not yet have a password, go to step 5.

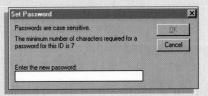

5 Enter a new password in the Set Password dialog box. There will be a minimum number of characters you must enter when creating the password. In this case it is seven characters. This limit is set by your Notes administrator.

6 Confirm the new password by entering it again in the next Set Password dialog box. Click on OK and then on Done in the User ID dialog box to close all the dialog boxes.

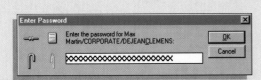

7 To clear your password, choose File, Tools, User ID, and enter the password for your user ID.

How to View and Lock Your User ID

You can view information about your user ID, including the basic settings, what certificates are in your user ID and the expiration date of the certificates, and any encryption keys you use to encrypt document fields. You can also access myriad options for sending ID information and requesting name changes or certificates. In addition, you can tell Notes to lock your user ID, which clears your user ID information and forces Notes to prompt for a user ID password when Notes is accessed again. This is useful when you leave your workstation temporarily and want to prevent others from using Notes with your user ID at your workstation.

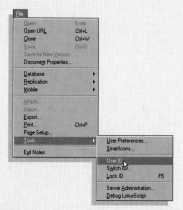

▶ **1** To view information about your user ID, choose File, Tools, User ID. If you have not password-protected your ID, skip to step 3.

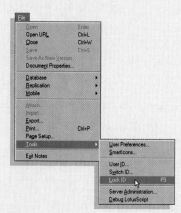

9 To lock your ID, choose File, Tools, Lock ID, or press F5. This will clear your user ID information and require you to re-enter your password the next time you access Notes.

8 Your user ID has a unique public encryption key that is used when you access a server and encrypt mail. To create a new public key (if you believe the security of your public key has been compromised, or if your ID was lost) click on New Public Key under Public Key Options. To mail your public key to a Notes administrator, click on Mail Public Key. To copy your Public Key to the clipboard so you can paste it somewhere else, click on Copy Public Key.

TIP SHEET

▶ **Your public key is unique to your user ID. Notes uses the key to authenticate that it is you who is accessing a Notes server. The public key is also used when you request to encrypt outgoing mail. Your public key is stored in your user ID and in your Person document in your Public Name and Address Book.**

▶ **You can switch to another user ID without exiting Notes. This is useful when you are sharing your workstation with another user or when you have more than one user ID file. To switch between user ID files, choose File, Tools, Switch ID and select a user ID file to switch to.**

2 Enter the password for your user ID.

3 You can see basic information about your ID, such as whether it is an International or North American type, as well as the type of Notes license it is used with: Lotus Notes, Notes Mail, or Notes Desktop. You can also tell if the ID is hierarchical or flat by looking at the ID type.

4 To see information about the certificates attached to your user ID, select Certificates on the left of the User ID dialog box.

5 You can delete a certificate from your ID by clicking on Delete. You can request a new certificate by clicking on Request Certificate (covered in detail on the next page). You can request a cross certificate by clicking on Request Cross Certificate (also covered in detail on the next page). Select a certificate under Certificates to display the creation and expiration date of the certificate in the lower half of the dialog box.

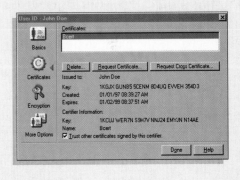

7 Click on More Options to see additional options such as to request a user ID name change. To create a safe copy of your ID to mail to a Notes administrator, click on Create Safe Copy. To merge one copy of your user ID with another user ID, click on Merge A Copy.

6 You can see any encryption keys stored in your ID by selecting Encryption. You can create a new encryption key by clicking on New, delete a key by clicking on Delete, mail a key to another user by clicking on Mail, export a key by clicking on Export, or import a key into your user ID by clicking on Import.

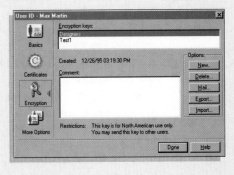

How to Request a New Certificate or a Name Change

A certificate is added to your user ID by a certifier ID and then stored in your user ID to be used to access Notes servers. When you first attempt to access a Notes server, the server makes sure you have a certificate in common with the certificates the server's Notes ID contains. If there is a certificate in common, you are granted access to the server; otherwise you are denied access to the server. You can examine the certificates stored in your user ID, request a new certificate or cross certificate, add a new certificate to your user ID, or delete a certificate from your user ID. You can also request to change the name assigned to your user ID.

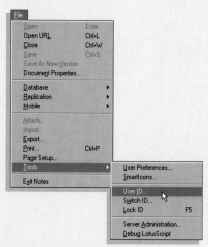

1 In order to carry out any actions involving certificates, first choose File, Tools, User ID, then enter your password (if you have password-protected your user ID) and click on OK.

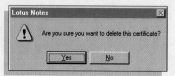

8 You may want to delete a certificate from your ID when it expires or when you are not using it any longer. To do this, choose File, Tools, User ID, then click on Certificates. Select the certificate you want to delete and click on Delete. Click on Yes when Notes asks you to confirm the deletion. *Note: This action cannot be undone!*

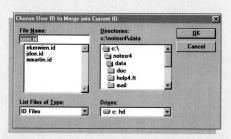

7 Click on Merge A Copy, then select the user ID you want to merge with your ID file. Click on OK (Open on the Macintosh) and then on Done in the User ID dialog box.

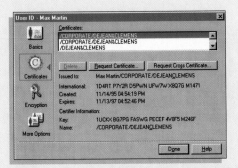

2 Select Certificates in the User ID dialog box.

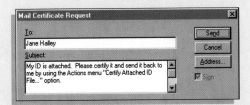

3 To request a new certificate from this dialog box, click Request Certificate. You will need the name of the person who can certify your user ID. They will use a file called a *certifier ID* to certify your ID. Enter the person's name in the To text box, then click on OK to mail it.

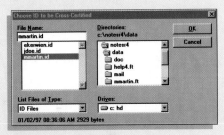

4 If your organization uses hierarchical naming, you may need a cross certificate to access one or more servers in a different part(s) of the organization. In this case, you want to request a cross certificate by clicking Request Cross Certificate. Select the ID you want to cross certify and click on OK (click on Open on the Macintosh).

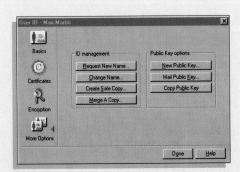

6 To add (merge) a certificate to your user ID, choose File, Tools, User ID, then click on More Options.

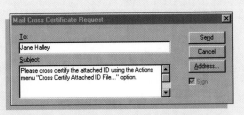

5 Enter the name of the Notes administrator in the To text box. Click on Send, and then click on Done in the User ID dialog box.

How to Secure a Local Database

You always have Manager access to a local database (a database stored on your workstation). You may want to secure the database so that other users cannot access it from your workstation, or copy the database to another disk from the operating system level to view it elsewhere.

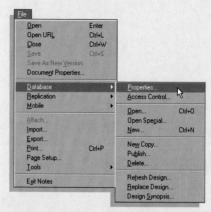

▶ **1** To encrypt a local database, select the database icon you want (on the workspace), or open it, and choose File, Database, Properties.

2 Click on the Encryption button.

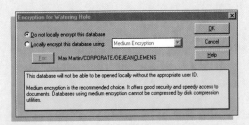

3 Select the Locally Encrypt This Database Using option.

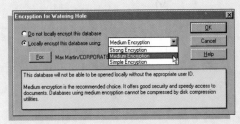

4 Next to the Locally Encrypt This Database Using option, choose Simple, Medium, or Strong Encryption. Strong and Medium Encryption are the most secure settings, however, it takes longer to open documents with these two settings. You also cannot use disk compression utilities on databases encrypted at these two settings. Simple encryption is less secure, but documents open faster and the database can be compressed using disk compression utilities.

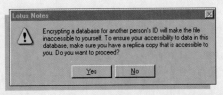

5 When you encrypt a local database, your current user ID is automatically chosen as the user ID that will be able to use the database. If you want to use another user ID to encrypt the database, click on the For button. Be aware that by doing this the database will become inaccessible to the current user ID. Notes opens your Name and Address Book(s) so you can choose another person's name (user ID) to encrypt the database.

6 To decrypt a database, open it with the user ID to encrypt it and choose File, Database, Properties. Click on the Encryption button and select Do Not Locally Encrypt This Database.

How to Encrypt Documents in a Shared Database

A database designer can create a form that encrypts one or more fields of a resulting document. In order to view data in an encrypted field, you must have the specific encryption key (also called a secret key) used for the document, provided to you by the database designer. Similarly, your Person document in your Public Name and Address Book contains your public encryption key, used primarily to encrypt your mail documents.

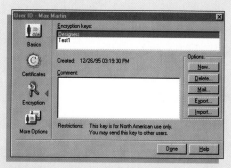

▶ **1** To create an encryption key (secret key), choose File, Tools, User ID and then enter your password if your user ID is password-protected. When finished, click on Encryption.

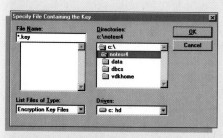

8 When someone sends you an encryption key, merge it with your user ID by choosing File, Tools, User ID. Enter your password, click on Encryption, and then click on Import. Find the location of the encryption file sent to you and click on OK (or Open on the Macintosh or Windows 95). If there is a password associated with the key, enter it, then click on Merge to add the key to your user ID.

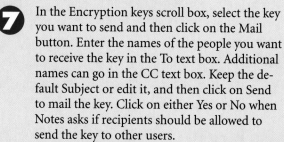

7 In the Encryption keys scroll box, select the key you want to send and then click on the Mail button. Enter the names of the people you want to receive the key in the To text box. Additional names can go in the CC text box. Keep the default Subject or edit it, and then click on Send to mail the key. Click on either Yes or No when Notes asks if recipients should be allowed to send the key to other users.

TIP SHEET

▶ **You have a public encryption key stored in your Person document in the Public Name and Address Book. This encryption key is not the same encryption key used specifically to encrypt fields in a document. Encryption (secret) keys are created specifically for encrypting document fields and must be distributed to one or more users.**

▶ **Encryption keys are also referred to as secret keys. When a designer has encrypted one or more fields of a document, you must first obtain the secret key from the designer (or a Notes administrator, depending on who is distributing it) before you can view encrypted data in these fields.**

▶ **You can delete an encryption key from your user ID. Choose File, Tools, User ID, enter your password, select Encryption, select the key, and click on Delete.**

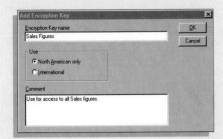

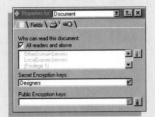

Click on the New button and enter the name of the key. Under Use select either North American Only or International. North American encryption keys can only be used by North American Notes users; International keys can be used by both North American and International users. North American encryption is more complex than International encryption due to current export limitations.

When you have at least Author access to a database, you can encrypt a document using either a secret encryption key or a public encryption key in a Public Name and Address Book. To encrypt a document using a secret encryption key, choose File, Document Properties.

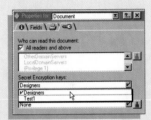

Select one or more secret encryption keys from the Secret Encryption Key option. Make sure there is a checkmark to the left of the key name, indicating that it is selected.

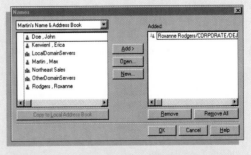

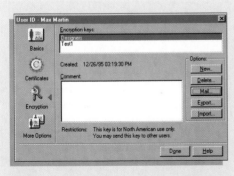

To mail a secret encryption key to another user, choose File, Tools, User ID, then click on Encryption.

To use one or more public encryption keys, select the Person icon next to the Public Encryption Keys option, the choose one or more names from the Names dialog box. When you are done adding names, click on OK. You can use both secret and public encryption keys for a single document.

CHAPTER 19

Browsing the World Wide Web with Notes

 The World Wide Web (or Web) is the graphical segment of the Internet. To understand more about the Web and the Internet, refer to *How To Use the Internet* from Ziff-Davis Press, or the myriad other books that cover this subject. You can browse the Web with Notes, either with a direct connection to the Internet or through an internet server or a Notes server that has a connection to the Internet.

The database that allows you to access the Web from Notes is called the Web Navigator. To access the Web using Notes, you can use a Server Web Navigator that resides on a Notes server with a connection to the Internet, or a Personal Web Navigator that relies on a direct connection to the Internet from your workstation.

You can browse the Web using the Web Navigator whether or not you are connected to the Internet. This is useful when you are on the road and want to read Web pages already stored in the Web Navigator database. To browse the Web while disconnected you must have either your Personal Navigator database or a local replica of the Server Web Navigator on your workstation.

You can also browse the Web from any database in Notes, or specify that Notes use another browser such as Netscape Navigator or Microsoft Internet Explorer. You can open a Web page from the File menu, the Search bar, by using a SmartIcon, from a Notes document, or from the Quick Search feature in the view pane of any database.

How to Set Up the Server Web Navigator

The Server Web Navigator allows you to access information on the Web through a Notes server (or InterNotes server; a Notes server connected to the Internet is referred to as an InterNotes server). The Server Web Navigator is a database that stores Web pages retrieved by all the users who access this database. The Server Web Navigator is also a shared database that can be used by anyone who has sufficient access to the database (as defined in the ACL of the database).

TIP SHEET

▶ If you are on the road and want to browse the Web using the Server Web Navigator (or the Personal Navigator), set the Retrieve/Open Pages option in your current Location document to No Retrievals so you will be able to open Web pages that have been stored in the Web Navigator. You can retrieve new Web pages when you reestablish a connection to the Internet.

▶ A *proxy server* is a server that allows Internet access to pass through it. A proxy server is usually set up between a local area network and direct Internet access.

▶ *Java* is a programming language that developers use to create *applets*. A Java applet is a small program, embedded in a Web page's source (HTML) document, that performs a task when a user accesses the Web page (or clicks on the applet while viewing the page).

▶ Check with your Notes administrator to be sure your workstation has the system requirements, including enough memory, to use the Server Web Navigator.

▶ **1** To set up and use the Server Web Navigator, first make sure you have all the system requirements with your Notes administrator. If you have all the necessary requirements, you are ready to edit (or create) a Location document in your Personal Name and Address book (choose File, Mobile, Edit Current Location; or File, Mobile, Locations).

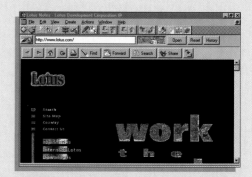

6 When you click on OK, Notes adds the Server Web Navigator database icon to your workspace and also opens the Web page you requested via the URL.

2 Under Internet Browser, choose From InterNotes Server in the Retrieve/Open Pages field. This will allow the InterNotes server to retrieve Web pages and store them in the Server Web Navigator. Click on the button to the right of the field to choose from three options. Make sure that Notes is selected in the Internet Browser field, so that you can see the Retrieve/Open Pages field.

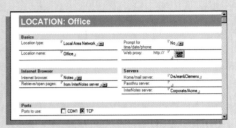

3 In the InterNotes Server field, enter the hierarchical name (for example, Corporate/Acme) of the InterNotes server where the Server Web Navigator database resides. If you connect to the Internet through a proxy server, enter the name or IP address of the proxy server in the Web Proxy field in the Basics section at the top of the Location document. (You will need to obtain this information from your Notes or network administrator.) This feature allows you to open Web pages that contain Java applets.

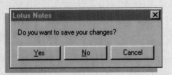

4 Close and save your Location document by pressing Esc and clicking on Yes. Make this location the current location (if it is not already).

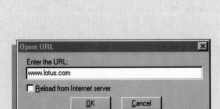

5 To easily add the Server Web Navigator database to your workspace, choose File, Open URL from your Notes workspace and enter the URL (Universal Resource Locator) for a Web page into the Open URL dialog box.

How to Set Up the Personal Web Navigator

The Personal Web Navigator is a database that resides on your local workstation and allows you to connect to the Web directly, assuming your workstation has a direct connection to the Internet. This is your own personal database (not shared) for browsing and storing Web pages. You can use it when you are connected to the Internet as well as when you are disconnected or on the road.

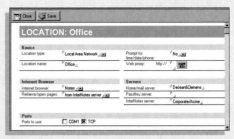

❶ To set up and use the Personal Web Navigator database on your workstation, you must first make sure you have all the system requirements with your Notes administrator. If you have all the necessary requirements, you are ready to edit (or create) a Location document in your Personal Name and Address book (choose File, Mobile, Edit Current Location; or File, Mobile, Locations).

2 Under Internet Browser, choose From Notes Workstation in the Retrieve/Open Pages field so that your workstation retrieves and stores Web pages in the Personal Web Navigator. Click on the button to the right of the field to choose from three options. Make sure that Notes is selected in the Internet Browser field, so that you can see the Retrieve/Open Pages field.

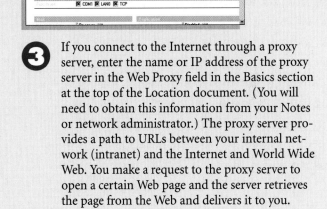

3 If you connect to the Internet through a proxy server, enter the name or IP address of the proxy server in the Web Proxy field in the Basics section at the top of the Location document. (You will need to obtain this information from your Notes or network administrator.) The proxy server provides a path to URLs between your internal network (intranet) and the Internet and World Wide Web. You make a request to the proxy server to open a certain Web page and the server retrieves the page from the Web and delivers it to you.

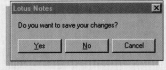

4 Close and save your Location document by pressing Esc and clicking on Yes. Make this location the current location (if it is not already).

6 Notes automatically adds the Personal Web Navigator database icon to your workspace and opens the Web page you requested in the Open URL dialog box.

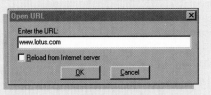

5 Choose File, Open URL from your Notes workspace. Enter the URL for a Web page, for example "www.lotus.com."

How to Use the Web Navigator and Browse the Web

You can browse the Web using the Web Navigator or through a number of other ways. You can open a Web page in several ways: from the File menu, from the Search bar, using a SmartIcon, from the Quick Search dialog box, or from an open Notes document.

1 To browse the Web using the Personal Web Navigator, open it from the workspace by double-clicking on the database icon.

9 You can open a Web page from the SmartIcons bar by clicking on the SmartIcon that contains the Open URL icon.

8 To open a Web page from the Search bar, open a database and choose View, Search Bar. Click on the icon to the left of the text box to display the Open URL icon. Enter the URL and click on Open.

7 To open a Web page from the File menu (from anywhere in Notes), choose File, Open URL and then enter the URL for the Web page you want to open.

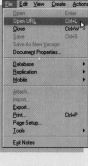

2 The Personal Web Navigator has views and folders to help you manage and locate Web pages. The All Documents view displays all the Web pages you have retrieved. When you drag a Web page from the view pane over the Bookmarks folder, you create a *bookmark* that will allow you quick access to the page the next time you want to open it.

3 Under Other (in the navigation pane), open the File Archive view to display Web pages with file attachments. Open the House Cleaning view to display Web pages based on their size. You can then reduce one or more Web pages to just their URLs by selecting the Web page(s) and clicking on Reduce To Link (on the Action bar). Open the Web Tours view to display Web Tour documents you have created. To create a Web Tour, browse the Web and open Web pages, then choose Actions, History to save those pages as a Web Tour.

4 To browse the Web using the Server Web Navigator, double-click on the Server Web Navigator database icon in the workspace, thereby opening the home page of the Server Web Navigator. The Our Home button opens your organization's home page on the Web.

6 The Sampler buttons open lists of Web pages that are categorized by topic. For example, click on Art And Culture to view a list of Web pages relating to this topic.

5 On the bottom of the home page are buttons that carry out various tasks. For example, click on Database Views to open the View navigator and browse Web pages stored in the database (as shown in this figure). Click on Recommended to display rated Web pages. Click on Directory Search to open a search form to carry out a search on the Internet using several Internet search engines. Click on Open URL to open a Web page with its URL. Click on User's Guide to open online help for the Web Navigator.

INDEX

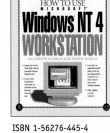

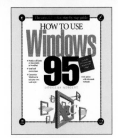

TRAINING

LEARN FROM THE EXPERTS

ERIC MANN
Lotus Certified Professional

Eric Mann is president of *WorkGroup Systems, Inc.* He spent more than six years at *Lotus Development Corporation* in the roles of *System Engineer* and *Major Account Executive*. In addition to consulting and teaching. His customer experiences provide Eric with a breadth of knowledge that will deliver vision and practicality in the deployment and use of Lotus Notes.

NOTES® 4.0 SYS ADMIN

- Level 1 ....$89.95
- Level 2 ....$89.95   **ALL 4 VIDEOS**
- Level 3 ....$89.95   **$329.95**
- Level 4 ....$89.95

Level 1 Course:	Level 2 Course:	Level 3 Course:	Level 4 Course:
• What is Notes?	• Expand Network	• Server Setup	• Troubleshooting
• Installing	• Setup	• Connecting	• Management
• Planning	• Security	• Replication	Techniques
• Server Setup		• Routing	
• Video Length–2 hrs	• Video Length–2 hrs	• Video Length–2 hrs	• Video Length–2 hrs

NOTES® 4.0 APP/DEV L-1

- Level 1 ....$89.95
- Level 2 ....$89.95   **ALL 3 VIDEOS**
- Level 3 ....$89.95   **$229.95**

Level 1 Course:	Level 2 Course:	Level 3 Course:
• What is Notes?	• Subforms	• Action & Views
• Creating Forms	• Inheritance	• Fields
• Creating Views	• Formulas	• Navigators
	• @ Functions	• Agents
• Video Length–2 hrs	• Video Length–2 hrs	• Video Length–2 hrs

NOTES® 4.0 END–USER

- Beginning $49.95
- Intermediate ....$49.95   **ALL 3 VIDEOS**
- Advanced $49.95   **$129.95**

Beginning Course:	Intermediate Course:	Advanced Course:
• Basic Concepts	• Getting Started	• Complex Documents
• Navigating	• Advanced Topics	• Programming
• Database Navigating	• Power Notes Mail	• Going Mobile
• Document Formatting		
• Video Length–2 hrs	• Video Length–2 hrs	• Video Length–2 hrs

NOTES® 4.0 DOMINO

- Essentials $89.95
-   **THIS VIDEO**
-   **$89.95**

Essentials Course:
- • What is Domino?
- • Home Pages
- • Navigators
- • Access Control
- • Video Length–1.5 hrs

FREE
DEMO VIDEO OR CD-ROM

FREE CATALOG AVAILABLE

FAX ►1•801•674•9734◄

LearnKey, Inc.
1845 W. Sunset Blvd, RM # 929
St. George, UT 84770

Dealer Inquiries Welcome

CALL NOW TO ORDER   www.learnkey.com

1•800•865•0165